LOVING HARDER

LOVING HARDER

OUR FAMILY'S ODYSSEY THROUGH ADOPTION
AND REACTIVE ATTACHMENT DISORDER

THE ORP LIBRARY

WRITTEN BY
LORI HETZEL
WITH
ALEKSANDRA CORWIN

WRITERS OF THE ROUND TABLE PRESS
PO BOX 511
HIGHLAND PARK, IL 60035

Publisher	COREY MICHAEL BLAKE
Executive Editor	KATIE GUTIERREZ
Lead Editor	ALEKSANDRA CORWIN
Director of Operations	KRISTIN WESTBERG
Facts Keeper	MIKE WINICOUR
Cover Design	ANALEE PAZ
Interior Design and Layout	SUNNY DIMARTINO
Proofreading	JONATHAN HIERHOLZER
Last Looks	NANCY YEANG
Digital Book Conversion	SUNNY DIMARTINO
Digital Publishing	SUNNY DIMARTINO

Printed in the United States of America
First Edition: September 2015
10 9 8 7 6 5 4 3 2 1

Library of Congress Cataloging-in-Publication Data
Hetzel, Lori
Loving harder: our family's odyssey through adoption and reactive
attachment disorder / Lori Hetzel.—1st ed. p. cm.
Print ISBN: 978-1-939418-74-6   Digital ISBN: 978-1-939418-75-3
Library of Congress Control Number: 2015945005
Number 12 in the series: The ORP Library
The ORP Library: Loving Harder

RTC Publishing is an imprint of Writers of the Round Table, Inc.
Writers of the Round Table Press and the RTC Publishing logo
are trademarks of Writers of the Round Table, Inc.

CONTENTS

To my family—

My loving husband, Karl
My children—Logan Karl, Connor Dane, Delaney Diana,
and Nadya Hope

INTRODUCTION

Today, according to the U.S. Department of Health and Human Services, more than 5.5 million children—or eight percent of kids—in the U.S. have some form of disability. Whether the problem is physical, behavioral, or emotional, these children struggle to communicate, learn, and relate to others. While there is no longer *segregation* in the same sense as there was in the 1950s, what remains the same is the struggle. Even with all of our resources and technology, parents of children with disabilities fight battles every day to find the help and education their children need.

I have led Oconomowoc Residential Programs (ORP) for almost thirty years. We're a family of companies offering specialized services and care for children, adolescents, and adults with disabilities. Too often, when parents of children with disabilities try to find funding for programs like ours, they are bombarded by red tape, conflicting information, or no information at all, so they struggle blindly for years to secure an appropriate education. Meanwhile, home life, and the child's wellbeing, suffers. In cases when parents and caretakers have exhausted their options—and their hope—ORP is here to help. We felt it was time to offer parents a new, unexpected tool to fight back: stories that educate, empower, and inspire.

The original idea was to create a library of comic books that could empower families with information to reclaim their rights. We wanted to give parents and caretakers the information they need to advocate for themselves, as well as provide educators and therapists with a therapeutic tool. And, of course, we wanted to reach the children—to offer them a visual representation of their journey that would show that they aren't alone, nor are they wrong or "bad" for their differences. What we found in the process of writing original stories for the comics is that these journeys are too long, too complex, to be contained within a standard comic. So what we are now creating is an ORP library of disabilities books—traditional books geared toward parents, caretakers, educators, and therapists, *and* comic books portraying the world through the eyes of children with disabilities. Both styles of books share what we have learned while advocating for families over the years while also honestly highlighting their emotional journeys. We're creating communication devices that anyone can read to understand complex disabilities in a new way.

In an ideal situation, these books will be used therapeutically, to communicate the message, and to help support the work ORP and companies like ours are doing. The industry has changed dramatically and is not likely to turn around any time soon—certainly not without more people being aware of families' struggles. We have an opportunity to put a face to the conversation, reach out to families, and start that dialogue.

Caring for children with disabilities consumes your life. We know that. And we want you to realize, through these stories, that you are not alone. We can help.

Sincerely,
Jim Balestrieri
CEO, Oconomowoc Residential Programs
www.orplibrary.com

A NOTE ABOUT THIS BOOK

Complex trauma and reactive attachment disorder are conditions that affect children in different ways. The child in the following story struggles with significant emotional and behavioral difficulties that require short-term placement in a specialized therapeutic environment. Many children with complex trauma do not resemble the child shown in this story. However, those who are similar to Nadya face challenges that make it difficult to benefit from special education in a traditional public school setting. Genesee Lake School strives to build relationships with the children in its care so that they learn new skills that will lead to a successful transition back to their homes, schools, and communities. It is our hope that the following story will add to your own understanding of the often lonely journey experienced by families with children with these unique challenges and gifts.

FOREWORD

Every once in a while, we encounter someone who changes our life forever. Lori Hetzel—a wife and mother of four, the author of *Loving Harder*, my adoption coordinator, and, most importantly, my friend—changed my life.

Lori walked every step of the way with me in my long journey to motherhood, encouraging me after an initial unsuccessful adoption and a country change. Finally, when the moment came and anxiety and panic suddenly consumed me, Lori never wavered in her loving patience and kindness to me during the most riveting and emotional experience of my life.

I've always believed there is an inextricable bond among adoptive parents because of the unique path we all must travel to parenthood. But the act of adopting is ultimately a moment of time that passes, and you then face the reality of parenting that child—*your* child—for a lifetime. My bond with Lori endures far beyond the moment when my dream was fulfilled and I became a mom to my beautiful son.

With unrelenting honesty, Lori has shared with me and many other adoptive parents *her* story as an adoptive mother through conversations, newsletters, or blogs. Lori happens to be not just an adoptive mother, but one whose daughter bears the indelible marks of nearly nine years of orphanage life. Lori and her husband, Karl, believe that every child deserves a family, and they have walked the talk—adopting Nadya when she was nine years old and her chances of adoption were slim.

The love of a family alone does not always erase the physical, emotional, and behavioral losses children suffer from neglect. Adoption means parenting a child no matter their past. Adoption is not a fairytale—when the event of adoption passes, you are left to parent a child who, by the very nature of being adoptable, has already suffered loss. What do you do if your child does not connect with you, your family, or anyone else? What do you do if your child demonstrates inexplicable fits of rage or does not "catch up" cognitively, socially, or even physically with her age peers? And what do you do when you find yourself questioning why you, why this child, and loathing the exhaustion, sadness, and resentment you feel building up toward your own child?

Lori shares her family's continuing journey with RAD with stark honesty and loving humor, never flinching from the poignant highs, excruciating lows, and hard-earned lessons learned. Lori's book provides inspirational insight that connects with adoptive parents and will give them practical guidance and hope. For any adoptive parent, *Loving Harder* is a true must-read.

Lori changed *our* lives. I am simply a mom who happened to adopt her son and who happens to be adopted, too. Because of Lori and her unwavering encouragement and support, we are now a happy family of three. For that support, my husband and I will forever be grateful to Lori, and my connection with her continues as friends and mothers. She is a source of profound wisdom and candor, and has taught me so much about being a mother. Thank you to my dear friend, Lori, for your kindness and generosity of spirit in sharing your story so that we can learn from you and with you.

Sherry Wheeler
Washington, D.C.

CHAPTER 1
ADOPTION IS LOVE

As our driver turned onto a single potholed lane and drove through a spiked wrought iron gate, the orphanage came into view. A wave of déjà vu overcame me as I stared at the featureless two-story Soviet-era building outside our frosty car window. *This is the baby home*, I thought, letting it sink in that we were finally here. The building matched the flat gray of the overcast October sky, but the window frames had been painted white a long time ago, making the cracks and peeling paint more noticeable. Karl squeezed my hand as the driver shut off the engine.

"Ready?" The translator provided by our adoption agency turned to us as if we were about to go on a carnival ride. *Ready*, I repeated silently, as though you can ever be truly ready for a moment like this. I looked at the panels of iron grating bolted to all of the windows, nodded, and opened my door.

I barely felt the cold as our translator and the in-country associate from our adoption agency guided us to the entrance. The landing was enclosed by an ornately carved wooden banister and capped off by a distinctive, sloped, gray tiled roof. It looked as though it could have been the entrance to a gingerbread house, and seemed out of place before the concrete building. I placed my hand on the doorknob, caught a glimpse of the lace curtains hanging inside, and froze.

"Go, go, Lori," motioned our translator, urging me to push the door open.

"I can't," I said, unable to move. "I've been here before."

"Ah," nodded our translator knowingly. "Déjà vu."

But I knew that my feeling was far more than that—to me, it was a sign of God's guiding hand. For the first time since we had accepted this blind referral, I was absolutely certain that we were in the right place. My excitement started to eclipse my apprehension.

We were one of the first American families to adopt from Kazakhstan since the country opened its doors to foreign adoption, but its system was still underdeveloped. A blind referral meant we did not receive a picture or specific profile of the child we were to adopt, but were guaranteed that one who met our general criteria (a girl between two and three years old) was available. For the last ten months, ever since Karl and I had decided that the time was finally right to expand our brood, we'd known next to nothing about the newest member of our family. Our two wonderful biological boys, Logan and Connor, were thirteen and seven. They waited for us with their grandparents back home in Milwaukee, Wisconsin, and they were just as excited and curious to meet their new sister as we were.

Karl and I had spent countless nights listening to our adoption anthem, "Somewhere Out There," from the animated movie *An American Tail*. I went through my days knowing there was a little girl, our daughter, somewhere out there, looking up at the same sky. I always knew what time it was in Kazakhstan and would wonder what she was doing at that moment. I would see her starting her day, and I wondered what her life looked like, what she had for breakfast, whether anyone read her a bedtime story. After so many months of wondering and longing to hold this unknown precious love, I was about to meet her.

With a pounding heart, I stepped into the lobby. I inhaled sharply and froze again when I saw the large carved wooden bear off to one side, framed by cream-colored lace curtains.

"It's exactly like in my dream," I whispered in Karl's ear. Just before leaving Wisconsin, I had dreamed this scene. Now, after forty-eight hours of travel, less than twenty-four hours in the country, and one completely sleepless night, we were about to meet our little girl. Again, I felt a strong sense of God's role in all of this.

I come from a large family of brown-haired, blue-eyed children, and yet my mother, one of only two in our family with brown eyes, had told me in recent years that she saw me holding a brown-eyed daughter in her dreams. She knew I had always longed to adopt. With the paycheck from my first job at age fifteen, I had signed up to donate twenty dollars a month to World Vision, an organization that feeds children in Africa. For as long as I could remember, my heart had ached at stories of hungry, neglected children, and Karl was the same; we had talked about our desire to help them from the moment we started dating.

Like me, Karl came from a large family of modest means but had been donating to children's charities as long as he had been earning money. He worked for a telecom company but volunteered at church on the weekends, and together we dreamed of a mixed family of biological and adopted children. He was the perfect match for me. Together, we set aside money every month for our favorite charities that supported children overseas, and we sent care packages every Christmas. Pursuing this international adoption was a natural extension of sharing our love in the world.

The orphanage director, a woman in her mid-forties whom I knew was also a pediatric neurologist, greeted us warmly in the lobby, shaking our hands and smiling widely. Her name was Irina, and she invited us all to sit down in her office where she quickly explained what would happen next. We would be taken to a roomful of children, she said, but there were only two girls who were in the age range we wanted and who were available for adoption. She said she would point them out to us once we got there. Irina reached into a small crystal bowl on her desk and picked up a piece of hard candy, orange with a clear plastic wrapper, and placed it in my palm. She said I was to give it to the child we wished to adopt, and that I should take care not to let the other children see it. Before I had a chance to respond, everyone stood up.

Karl and I gave each other a wary look as we all followed Irina down the hall, our steps echoing loudly on the cold tile floors. I gripped the piece of candy in one hand as Karl and I held on to each other, hearts racing.

One of the last times I had taken my mother shopping before she passed away from cancer, we had stumbled into the children's clothing section. Like any two women in this situation, we started pointing out our favorite outfits to each other, just because.

"Oooh, look at this one," I cooed, holding up an adorable white cotton sundress with pink ribbon trim. "And this one!"

My mother laughed, and the sound warmed me. "Would you just adopt already?" she demanded in mock exasperation. "I want my brown-eyed granddaughter!"

As we walked down the hall, I knew my mother was smiling down on our leap of faith and love. I was equally sure that the brown-eyed granddaughter she had seen in her dream was behind one of these closed doors. I was only sorry they would never meet. My mother had passed just a few months before we received approval for our international adoption.

Karl hummed the Steven Curtis Chapman song "When Love Takes You In," just loud enough for me to hear. The song describes the miracle of hope a family can bring to an orphaned child, and the first time he played it for me, emotion filled his eyes.

Irina opened a door toward the end of the long hallway and stepped inside, beckoning us to follow. We found ourselves at the back of a large rectangular room, where about a dozen children under the age of five sat in rows of low chairs facing a small stage, watching a puppet show put on by staff members. The floor was covered with ornate floral carpeting in pastel colors, and a row of tall mirrors against one wall made the room feel surprisingly bright. The windows were clean, and a baby grand piano was tucked in one corner along with a few bins of instruments and toys. We quietly sat down in the last row to observe.

For the most part, the children were dressed in layers of mismatched clothes that, while not completely worn out, were not their Sunday best, either. Irina pointed to two women sitting next to each other on one side of the room. Each held a tiny girl in her lap, and each girl wore a dress and bow in her scanty wisps of hair for the special presentation day. The women turned slightly so that we could get a better look. The younger of the two children was clearly too young for what our family was hoping for—she could barely stand on her own. While most couples that adopt do so because they cannot have children of their own and want the experience of raising a baby, we already had our boys and wanted our adoption to focus on slightly older children whom we knew were often overlooked. The other little girl was around two and a half, brown eyed and laughing at the puppet show. As soon as we saw her, we knew.

I looked down at the hard orange candy in my hand and gave Karl a worried look. This process was heartbreaking, as though they were asking us to choose a puppy from a litter. I also thought a hard candy could be a choking hazard to such a small child, but Irina motioned to the woman holding the little girl and she stood to make her way over to us. The little girl looked up at us with the most beautiful doe-eyed angel face and then turned away again, probably frightened by the two new faces, and also by the fact that she rarely saw men. Karl and I held still for several moments, taking her in. Her hair was cropped close to her head, with a few wispy bangs in front—I had no idea how the two enormous red and white ribbons on either side of her head stayed put. She was wearing a baby-blue dress with long white sleeves and an enormous white needlepoint collar that came halfway down her chest. She had plump round cheeks and a perfect button nose. She was so small she could have been half her age. We were completely smitten.

She looked at us warily from the arms of her caretaker. Gently, I reached over to stroke her back; I was already falling in love.

At the time, I worked as an assistant in a dental office, and I frequently worked with children. One of my favorite things to do was to take on different characters and accents to take the children's minds off the scary business of dentistry. Putting kids at ease was one of my specialties, and parents often specifically requested me for their children's cleanings for that reason. How I wished this precious Kazakh girl could understand me as I softly told her how we would like to be her new family and promised I would take good care of her. I thought about how I would love to hold and rock her and make her laugh. I just stroked her hair and back, brimming with tears as Karl and I locked eyes in a moment of complete understanding and love—this was our daughter.

Her caretaker gently handed her over to us, and I took her in my arms like the treasure she was. She was frightened and I'm sure overstimulated by the strange way we looked and smelled, so I held her for just a moment before pressing the candy into her hand. She took it gladly, and then looked anxiously back to her caretaker. Irina was waiting, so I handed the little girl back and in just five minutes it was all over. Our daughter and her caretaker sat back down, and Karl and I went to the office with overflowing hearts to complete the paperwork.

When we had jumped into the adoption process less

than a year before, we knew our path would take us overseas. While there are plenty of children in need in America, too, each family feels their own calling in this regard. We looked to orphanages in the East, which were dramatically understaffed and underfunded. Disproportionate numbers of children were being placed in mental institutions while still in grammar school because orphanages didn't have the resources to care for them, and these children would quickly turn to drugs and prostitution when they aged out, or even earlier if they ran away because of abuse. These were dire and hopeless situations, and we wanted to adopt a child who might otherwise be lost within them.

Our adoption agency proposed something we had never considered—to be one of the first families to adopt in Kazakhstan while using a blind referral. Situations like this aren't completely uncommon with countries that are just opening up to the West, and we jumped at the opportunity to make the adoption happen quickly. We took a crash course in Russian and picked out a name—Delaney. We were happy to be the guinea pig for this noble cause.

We spent three weeks bonding with Delaney—though often for only an hour a day. Each day, Irina would greet us and ask through the translator if we were rested and enjoying our time there.

"Da, spasibo," we would answer, which meant "Yes, thank you." She would take us to the same room, where a staff person was usually playing the piano while the children danced with each other. The first time we saw them paired up, our hearts melted.

That first day, we accompanied the group of children

on their daily walk outside. A nurse observed us as we observed Delaney. By and large, the children couldn't take their eyes off us, but Delaney was shy and hid behind her friends, only peeking out at us from time to time. Most of the children could dress themselves, but there were also staff members available to help them. The coats were too large for toddlers, falling past their knees. They didn't have boots, but they all had mittens and scarves and the grounds were clean except for a fine dusting of snow. As the children walked down the stairs, some tumbled because they couldn't see their feet. Unhurt, they would just roll down the shallow stairs to the ground in a way that was sweetly comical, laughing all the while. We kept our eyes closely on Delaney, and our translator gently asked her to walk nearer to us. One of the staff women tried to corral her from behind the other children, but she was shy and we didn't want to pressure her. I held out my hand, but she didn't take it, so we just strolled down the street alongside the children. Eventually, Delaney fell into step right behind us, which was enough for us. After we escorted the group back inside, we were told that was the end of our first day of bonding. We waved goodbye and the children enthusiastically waved back. I gave Delaney a little hug, and while she was apprehensive, she received it. We could barely sleep and continued thinking and talking about her throughout the night.

On the second day, we joined the children sitting on small chairs around low tables in the music room again. Delaney was more willing to engage with us as we played with the large colorful blocks set out on the tables. Irina said it was fine for me to share the box of cookies I had brought, and all the children gobbled them up. Delaney's eyes lit up as she reached for a cookie, giving us a big smile, and for the first time I realized she had two perfect dimples. Then the translator told us we could have our first private bonding session with Delaney, and they escorted us to a separate room where there was a small pit filled with colorful balls. Delaney jumped right in and we played with her, throwing balls back and forth. I pulled some Ritz crackers out of my purse and gave her one, after which she climbed right onto my lap, indicating she wanted more crackers. It was amazing to have my daughter on my lap for the first time, as she happily stuffed one cracker after another into her tiny mouth. The moment passed too quickly, and soon a staff member came to tell us our time was up.

On the third day, Delaney kissed me when I walked into the room, and smiled at Karl. Little by little, we could feel ourselves becoming a family.

After two weeks of bonding, we spent the last week formalizing the adoption in Kostanay, the small town on the northern border with Russia where the orphanage was located. Everything was new to us, and the culture shock was at times overwhelming. The apartment the orphanage liaison had arranged for us was gray and gloomy, like almost everything in Kazakhstan. The walls were old and cracked and our door had three massive deadbolts on it, which was not reassuring. Only rusty brown water drained from the pipes, but we didn't want to offend our orphanage representative by asking for different accommodations. Instead, we bought five-liter bottles of water and sponge-bathed and brushed our teeth as best we could. The highlight of each day was the time we got to spend playing games and cuddling with Delaney at the orphanage.

Finally, after three weeks, we were free to take Delaney out of the orphanage with us. She was comfortable with us by now, but she was still terrified of getting in the car, something she had never done, and screamed and cried as we tried to get her inside. She was too young to fully understand what was happening, but I had bonded with her enough to know that rocking and singing, along with chocolate chip cookies, would help soothe her. By the time we arrived back at the apartment, she was our happy smiling girl again.

The next day, the three of us flew to the capital of Almaty, located on the other side of the country. There, we needed to visit the US Embassy to receive paperwork that would allow us to take Delaney out of the country. We thought we would be in Almaty for two days, but the paperwork was not ready when we arrived, and the one person who could approve it had just gone on vacation. No one knew when he was coming back.

No adoption is without its hiccups, and we had come prepared with a cushion of money and time to account for them. Nonetheless, two days quickly stretched into a week, and we were in danger of running out of funds. We had spent nearly all our savings and were paying an outrageous sum to stay in a hotel in Almaty to do nothing but wait. We still had one more stop ahead of us in Moscow, where we would need to spend a few days visiting the US Embassy to acquire the visa Delaney would need to enter the US. We didn't know how we were going to make it or even if Karl would still have a job upon our return with the extra time he was taking off. The adoption agency representatives seemed vague and evasive when we spoke to them, but they were trying to do the best they could under our dire circumstance we faced. There really wasn't much they could do. It was a waiting game. We felt completely helpless and alone. To top it off, Connor was so ill with strep throat back home that he couldn't even talk on the phone, and his grandmother had to take him to the hospital for antibiotics. I was desperate to get back home to him. Karl lost twenty pounds during the trip from stress, yet we tried to keep our spirits up and prayed constantly. Our emotions were constantly conflicting and changing—one second joy and the next turmoil. We held on to each other and prayed for a resolution.

Just as we were at our wit's end, a young woman approached me in the hotel lobby and asked if we had just adopted the little girl with us. Karl was holding Delaney on his lap as we sat at a small table with our translator, having a beer. I was shocked to hear someone speak American English to me, and although I wanted to cleave to the comfort of a familiar language, I muttered a quick "No," and looked away. Taken aback, the woman apologized and then took a seat at a nearby table and opened her laptop.

From the moment we landed, the guide and the translator provided by our adoption agency had made us fearful about being "watched." They told us to keep a low profile because Kazakhstan was crawling with Russian mafia who might want to kidnap a child from an American couple and hold her for ransom. Our translator warned us repeatedly not to attract attention. At this point, the stress and intrigue were high, and we felt surrounded by strangers and unsure of when our issues would be resolved. I thought, *To heck with this! This is just what I've been praying for.* I grabbed my beer, stood up, and walked over to the woman's table without looking back at Karl or the translator.

I pulled up a chair and sat down across from her, apologizing for lying. I was choking back tears, couldn't swallow, and in a minute I was shaking and sobbing as I told her our story—that there seemed to be no end in sight to the delays, and that we were practically out of money. We had arrived in the country with almost $8,000 in cash, and now it was just about gone. I was afraid Karl would have to fly back to keep his job, and I would have to stay alone with Delaney to await a resolution.

The woman's name was Jenny, and she was a Christian missionary living in Kazakhstan. She placed her hand on my arm and, with the gentlest voice, told me not to worry—she knew our daughter was adopted, and she knew she had been guided to that hotel lobby for a reason, and now she knew why. That night, she picked us up at the hotel and brought us to her house for a spaghetti dinner. The next day, she and her husband Stewart cleared out one of their children's bedrooms to make room for us in their home. She insisted we stay with them for as long as we needed. Karl and I were in disbelief. I was sure that Jenny was a guardian angel sent to help us, especially when she revealed that she had taken a different route to work that morning; she didn't normally stop in that hotel but for some reason had felt compelled to do so that day.

It was such a relief to be surrounded by another American family. They had also adopted a little brown-eyed girl from Kazakhstan and had three biological boys that were close in age to our own, so we had plenty of similar experiences to talk about. Within a week, Jenny and Stewart had used their knowledge of the language and the system to sort out the mess we were in. In the end, we were stranded in Kazakhstan for over a month, when we thought the process would take less than three weeks. Without Jenny, I'm not sure how long we would have been there.

In spite of the high levels of anxiety, we were overcome with love for our little girl. She didn't speak much, but she was sweet and affectionate and we had learned enough Russian to communicate with her about her basic needs. The love that filled my heart for Delaney was unlike anything I had ever experienced. I was committed to being the best mother I could be to my daughter.

After a quick three days in Moscow to obtain Delaney's US visa, we finally boarded a plane home. We couldn't wait to see Connor and Logan and introduce them to their new sister. We felt truly blessed.

CHAPTER 2
OUR HEARTS WANT MORE

Becoming the mother of a daughter was one of the greatest joys of my life. It made me feel closer to my own mother, despite her absence. With four older brothers, I had shared a special bond with my mother, just like I did now with Delaney. I loved shopping with her, dressing her up—things I could never do with my boys. She was my heart. She still is.

Delaney integrated into our family without a hiccup. It took her a while to start speaking, but she was a sweet-natured child and loved being held. Connor and Logan doted on her, and Logan even babysat her on the weekends so Karl and I could go on date nights.

Of course, no child comes out of an orphanage system completely unscathed; some level of neglect is unavoidable most of the time, and even mild neglect can negatively affect a child's brain development, often leading to learning delays later in life. The Kazakh orphanage had told me Delaney was "retarded," but our adoption agency had warned us that the old Soviet system almost universally labeled their children in this way, meaning that the child was simply developmentally delayed in some respect. The agency added that these same children often thrived with loving, attentive families when brought to the US. That was the case with Delaney. Though we anticipated that she would have some learning delays once she hit school age, we understood that they were more directly related to the experience in an understaffed orphanage than to her intellectual capacity, and I was glad that I hadn't put too much stock in what the orphanage had claimed. I enrolled her in a regular preschool where she interacted well with other children and quickly caught up developmentally to children her age.

I had quit my job as a dental assistant to stay home and care for Delaney, but with such a positive overall experience behind us, the adoption agency asked if I could work as a liaison for other families considering adoption. I jumped at the chance to help other parents understand what they could expect when pursuing an adoption from Kazakhstan. I tried to prepare them for grueling travel and the expected costs, as well as the culture shock, but most importantly, I shared the wonderful stories of the Dolphin Baby House where we adopted Delaney, and how the care and attention the children received there far exceeded our expectations—the children did have a pool and a sauna, after all!

Soon, one of our neighbors adopted from Kazakhstan, and several other families I had spoken to were pursuing the same route. One day I was finally able to meet the agency director in person at an all-family adoption picnic. Right there, she asked me to join her company in a more expanded capacity.

"Every family you talk to ends up adopting from Kazakhstan!" she told me. "Would you be willing to be a case manager for us? Why not get paid for what you're already doing?"

I loved the idea, and began working from home nearly full-time as an advocate for parents going through the adoption process. There were mountains of paperwork to go through to fulfill adoption requirements, and I knew how difficult all the waiting and maneuvering of the system could be. One of the biggest pieces of the puzzle was getting a family's "home study" approved. This was a process that entailed coordinating with state social services to do a thorough evaluation of the home and family situation of the proposed adoptive family, to ensure they were stable and suitable. I helped families fill out forms, coordinated appointments with social workers, and prepared families for what they could expect over the next few weeks during the social worker's and state representative's visits. I also became a confidante and advisor to parents embarking on this journey, and a shoulder for them to cry on when things didn't go as planned.

During this time, we moved to Las Vegas. Immediately, we fell in love: no more harsh, restrictive, long winters—only blue skies, sun, mountains, and palm trees. We felt as though life was on a positive upswing, and we were positively gleeful.

The agency handled adoptions from an increasingly wider range of countries—including Russia, Ukraine, and China. As part of our adoption had been handled through the US Embassy in Moscow, giving me some familiarity with the Russian program, I was asked to take on the Russia portfolio in addition to Kazakhstan. Now a large part of my day was spent looking through profiles of children available for adoption and matching them with appropriate families.

Each of the caseworkers at our agency—there were about seven of us—worked with a particular set of families. Once I had obtained profiles of available Russian children, I would pass them on to the families in my charge who were anxious for information about their options.

Usually a family had three days after receiving a referral to decide whether to accept it. In that time, the family could contact a doctor if they chose and go over the medical profile and measurements of the child. Things like head circumference and distance between the eyes, small eye openings, flat upper lip below the nose, and where the ears lay were all informative signs. These facial features could indicate that the child was exposed to alcohol in utero, which can result in learning disabilities and behavioral and physical damage. Also investigated was whether the child had a history of hepatitis A, B, or C or exposure to syphilis, and whether those conditions were treated. Answers to these questions could indicate developmental problems that weren't reported in the written profiles. The work gave me an unprecedented sense of fulfillment and purpose.

Less than two years after we adopted Delaney, we started thinking that we would like a sister for her. Karl and I thought it would be nice if the two of them shared the common bond of adoption. During the agency's matching meetings, I kept seeing a shy, smiling face getting passed over for adoption, but nothing in her profile indicated why. Her name was Nadezhda, pronounced in English as Nadya, which means *hope*. She was six years old, and each time she was passed over, my heart broke a little for her.

"What's going on with Nadya?" Karl often asked me when he came home. He was supportive of my work and loved hearing the stories of children we successfully placed with families. Again and again, I gave him the sad update that she was still without a family.

"She looks like an angel," Karl said, looking at her picture. Her hair was blond and cut short, like a little boy's. She had piercing blue eyes and wore a large blue bow on top of her head. She had been in the orphanage since she was two months old. Her profile stated that she had a favorite caretaker, played with a doll, and was able to tie her shoes—all positive signs.

"Why isn't she getting adopted, Lori?" Karl asked. "What's wrong with her? She looks okay to me."

I leaned up against the wall in the entryway to the kitchen, where we stood. "I think most families are just scared of adopting a child over five, and that's pushing it. First-time families want babies. They don't want an older child. They want to experience infancy."

"I'm going to pray for her," Karl said. "Pray she finds a family to love her."

The next day, I came home from work to see that Karl had made Nadya's profile picture the background image on his computer screen.

"Why do you have Nadya on your computer screen?" I lingered as I passed his home workstation.

He turned around and stared at me with a wide, odd grin on his face, but said nothing.

"What are you thinking, Karl? You want us to adopt her, don't you?"

"Well, to be honest," he started, "I have been thinking about it . . ."

I shifted my weight and sighed quietly, not wanting to seem uncomfortable.

Karl went on. "What *if* we adopted Nadya? Couldn't she be the sister for Delaney? That common bond we discussed?"

Truth was, the idea had been bouncing around in my head as well. As most adoptive parents know, it's not hard to fall in love with a picture and a profile and to start imagining a happy, growing family with a child you've never met.

After a few moments of silence, Karl spoke again. "I think we have enough love in our family to take in this little girl, don't you think?"

"Yes," I said. "I think we do."

I had worked in the adoption field long enough to know that adopting an older child would come with distinctive challenges. It would change our solid family dynamic. In Las Vegas, we were thriving. The five of us went to church together on Sundays, often followed by a hotel on the strip downtown for brunch. Other weekends we would head out to Lake Las Vegas to watch the boats float by and enjoy our favorite ice cream. By this time, Delaney was almost five years old, and she was a bundle of joy and love.

I knew that the older children got, the more developmental challenges they had. Any adoptive family in the US has to watch online videos and attend a few seminars to demonstrate that they have been educated on common issues with adoptions, including attachment disorders and cognitive delays. I knew enough to know that after age five, the chances of having a severely traumatized child greatly increased.

"She will have needs," I continued to Karl, mulling the idea over out loud for the first time. "I will have to spend a lot of time with her, which will be hard on Delaney since she's the baby of the family." I struggled. Even though both Logan and Connor were older, they needed my attention too, and I knew this would split my focus from my other children. Nadya wouldn't know English and would have problems in school. She would have some attachment issues. I knew that.

"She just needs love," Karl said staunchly.

I looked at the wonderful, sensitive man who believed wholeheartedly that love could conquer all. I was tempted to agree with him. Still, a voice whispered warnings in the back of my mind.

"Love can't fix all children," I said. "Especially older, traumatized ones."

But we had spent much of the past year talking and thinking about Nadya, and it wasn't long after that before we started to think of her as part of the family.

One day, the Russian agency told us they were going to remove her from the database and place her in a mental institution. We were shocked, because while we knew this was a possibility for teenage children who weren't getting adopted, we didn't understand why Nadya would be facing this future. Typically, the only reason a younger child is placed in a mental institution is if he or she presents aggressive behavior, like pyromania, or has severe disabilities. There was no therapy available for such children. Worse, I knew that children in Russian mental institutions were often put on a cocktail of drugs that kept them subdued or even sedated, and many spent hours a day staring at a blank wall. I couldn't bear to think of this little girl experiencing that fate.

After a few days of conversation with Karl and constant ruminating on my own, I contacted my agency.

"Hi, this is Lori Hetzel," I greeted my supervisor. "I wanted to let you know that I found a family for Nadya."

"Really?" she replied, surprised. "Wow, that's great news! Which family is it?"

I took a deep breath as I paced my small home office. Before I could change my mind, I said, "Mine."

CHAPTER 3
THE RUSSIAN SYSTEM

Unlike our single-visit Kazakh experience, Russia would require two visits to complete the adoption process. The first trip was to formally accept our referral for Nadya and would include a limited period for bonding, and the second trip would be much shorter and would legally finalize the adoption. About a year after initiating the process, we received approval from the Russian agency to book our travel. The whole family would be coming, minus Logan, who was now a senior in high school and couldn't miss class. Connor and Delaney had their bags packed and were excited to fly to Siberia to meet their new sister.

Two days before our scheduled departure, we received a shocking email: there had been a terrible mix-up, said Olga, our in-country associate, and we were no longer allowed to come. The Ministry of Education, which oversees all adoptions, had notified the agency that Nadya was not, in fact, eligible for permanent adoption, and that the adoption should never have been approved. We were dumbfounded. How could this kind of mistake happen? I had never come across this kind of situation in my career. Our much-anticipated departure date came and went, and we stayed home, shocked and numb and answerless, believing our little girl had just slipped between our fingers.

A few weeks later, the situation became even more bizarre when we received an apologetic phone call from Olga, saying the Ministry of Education had made an error: the previous communication had actually been referring to a *different* Nadya and somehow the lines had gotten crossed. The Ministry of Education apologized profusely and said we were now allowed to come again, because our Nadya was still available for adoption.

Almost two months after our original departure date, we rebooked our tickets and were counting down the days to departure attempt number two. To our horror, three days before the flight, Olga emailed again to say that we couldn't come. Nadya had been taken off the database and was no longer available for adoption. I was sick about it. I stared at the words on the computer screen in disbelief. I couldn't get Nadya out of my head. I looked at our packed suitcases and cried.

Later on, we found out that the woman who was in charge of updating the database had been caught in a corruption scandal, accepting money in return for removing children from the database, although it was never exactly clear to what end. Because of a technicality (children had to be in the database for six months before they were eligible for adoption), we would have to wait another six months before we could potentially travel to Russia again.

We were prepared for difficulties, but we had now lost thousands of dollars for all the tickets, visas, and paperwork, and had no idea when the adoption would finally go through. In the meantime, we had moved to Texas for Karl's job with a new telecommunications firm, so we had to initiate the entire home study and adoption approval process for the state of Texas, starting from the beginning. There were times I cried with frustration in the middle of the night, thinking about all the delays and how helpless we felt as Nadya turned seven, then eight, then finally nine in the orphanage.

"Do you think this is some sort of . . . sign?" I asked Karl one day. "Maybe that we're not supposed to go? Maybe this is God telling us that this is not going to be good for us."

"It does seem strange," he agreed, and we didn't know what else to do except pray for guidance.

"God loves children," Karl said. "He says look out for widows and orphans. Adopting a child can never be a bad thing." We shook off our fears; faith and hope made us press on.

. . .

Karl and I finally boarded a plane in late November of 2006, almost three years after first seeing Nadya's picture. We held our breaths and prayed as the plane took off. From Moscow, we flew four hours east to Kemerovo, a small city in southern Siberia. Nadya's orphanage was in a tiny village called Inskoy, which was another two-hour drive south of Kemerovo, firmly planted in the middle of nowhere. Kemerovo was the nearest town with a hotel, so we stayed there and made the nerve-racking drive down potholed, two-lane roads with our driver each day.

Most of the drive took us through desolate, empty fields covered in heavy Siberian snow. Once we got closer to Inskoy, we passed through enormous forests of white birch trees, twinkling with snow and icicles, and there was a smattering of run-down homes with peeling paint and peaked roofs along the way. At the center of Inskoy, an enormous coal plant shot thick clouds of black smoke into the air from three massive smokestacks, and in the shadow of the billowing black cloud—the orphanage. Going from the pristine, shining birch forest to the industrial gloom of Inskoy so quickly was disconcerting. It was as though we had traveled from heaven to hell—and before I knew it, we were pulling up to the front gate.

The gray block building, crumbling in some corners, resembled an industrial park in the US and slightly reminded me of Delaney's orphanage. We were nervous—much more nervous than we had been with Delaney's adoption. The stakes seemed higher, the process had taken much longer, and we had already been through so much. As we approached the door, I could already pick up the distinctive smell of boiled cabbage, which I despised.

Our translator checked us in at the front desk while we smiled at the handful of children milling around the lobby, looking to see who had come in. The heating inside was kept at a bare minimum and the children were bundled up in layers of winter sweaters.

"Amerikanski! Amerikanski!" exclaimed one of the boys when he saw us. They piled into the doorway, giggling and fighting for a peek at the foreign visitors. They were also looking for candy or cookies, knowing American parents always traveled with treats.

The woman at the front desk shushed the boys and motioned for one of the girls to come closer. She said a few words to her in Russian and told us that this girl would escort us to the room where Nadya and her caretaker were waiting. We weren't surprised that they had a little orphaned girl doing the job of taking us to meet Nadya, as most orphanages are understaffed, but it was still heartbreaking.

The beanpole of a girl, about ten years old, had shoulder-length brown hair and wore a dark sweater and pink pants that were slightly flared at the bottom; they barely fit her, ending well above her ankle. She had on ankle socks and brown canvas shoes that looked as though they could have belonged to several other children before her. She silently nodded at the woman's instructions and looked over her shoulder to make sure we were following as she walked us down the hallway.

"Shhhh," Karl said to me in a low voice, sensing my emotion. He had been squeezing my hand from the moment we walked in, knowing how much more challenging this visit would be for us. "This is not like the baby home."

"I know," I said, trying to swallow past the lump in my throat. "I know."

Delaney's baby home had been full of hope—we knew walking in that all of the young children there had a good chance of being adopted. The children we saw here looked anywhere from ten to fourteen years old, and we passed some who were on their hands and knees, scrubbing the floors and radiators with stiff brushes. Others were sweeping or standing on chairs wiping windows. The tiles were worn through in certain places, revealing the underlying cement, but the place was clean, and the hallway freshly painted white. Walking slowly behind the sad brown-haired girl and knowing that all these children faced slim odds of escaping their circumstances was devastating. I saw their faces looking at us as we passed, and my body filled with guilt as I wondered what they were thinking. *How many families have come and passed them by, just as we are? How do these children feel about themselves? Do they feel that they are not good enough to be adopted? That there is something wrong with them? Why her? Not me?*

I had to blink the painful thoughts away.

The little orphan guide walked us to the door, paused, and pointed at it, giving us one last look as a tear rolled down her cheek. She quickly wiped it, then turned around and, without a backward glance, sulked away down the hall. I stared after her for a long moment, unable to begin to imagine what she was feeling, and my stomach twisted with a wretched, unfamiliar sadness.

"Here we go," said Karl as our translator held the door open for us. I wiped the wetness from my eyes, took a deep breath, and walked in.

The large classroom-type setting had children's chairs scattered around several large, ornate area rugs. Elegant wooden cabinets lined one wall, and murals of trees and scenes from Russian fairy tales adorned the others.

The orphanage director and our adoption agency's representative greeted us with warm smiles and enthusiastic handshakes. On the other side of the room, Nadya sat on the floor with her caretaker—one of the social workers at the facility—and a group of boys gathered behind us to peer through the crack in the door until the orphanage director muttered something to them and closed the door.

Nadya's social worker stood up and greeted us with a polite nod. Then she looked at Nadya, and Nadya quickly glanced in our direction and then back to the social worker. The woman inclined her head slightly towards us and gave Nadya a meaningful look. Instantly, Nadya turned and ran towards us.

"Mama! Papa!" she exclaimed, wrapping her legs around mine and looking up at me with shining blue eyes and a wide smile. My heart melted as I saw the excitement and happiness in her face. She glanced over her shoulder at her caretaker, as though looking for approval. There was something discomfiting about how Nadya seemed to have rehearsed this scene—no child would naturally offer up such affection to a stranger. But I didn't think she was entirely faking her excitement.

I knelt down beside her and looked into her eyes.

"Hello, Nadya," I said in Russian. "Nice to meet you."

She looked intensely, searchingly, at my face. I wasn't sure she understood what I was saying, and I wondered if my broken Russian was to blame.

I pulled a banana out of my purse and peeled it.

"I brought you a treat," I told her, assuming she had probably never seen a banana. She didn't know what to do with it, but she looked hungry. "You can eat it," I told her, using the Russian word for treat and indicating with my hand that she could put it in her mouth. Without a word, she opened her mouth wide and shoved the entire banana down her throat in one quick movement.

"Oh no!" I gasped, panicking and worried that she would choke. I stared at her wide-eyed as she chewed, and Karl chuckled.

"I guess she was hungry!" he laughed as Nadya smiled

at us through a mouthful of banana mush.

This is my child, I thought, already nervous that our time with her would be so short. *I have three days to establish some kind of relationship with her.* My throat tightened. The pressure to evaluate and bond with her in such a short period of time was intense. Most families in this situation feel that they've spent a small fortune to get there and recognize that if they decide the referral isn't the right fit, they may not get a second child to consider. We had roughly three hours, over three days, to decide. So many thoughts raced through my mind as I stroked her hair. *Am I going to be okay with this little girl? Is this going to work?*

Of course, I thought. *It has to work.*

We would not meet this child and leave without her. Who would do such a thing? I could not even fathom it. We would be fine.

• • •

Nadya was tiny as a sparrow; at nine years old, she looked like she was four. She probably didn't weigh more than forty pounds. She was dressed like a little boy in dark pants and a dark sweatshirt, with hair cropped short and jagged blond bangs cut high across her forehead. We suddenly felt that we were on a rescue mission, and the urgency to adopt her increased. She charmed us completely—taking us by the hands and parading us around the orphanage, showing us off to other kids as they peeked out of doorways to get a glimpse.

We spent our hour with her that first day trying to play different games and taking notes on what we observed. It was important for us to see how well she listened and what her level of physical coordination was. Children who have experienced severe developmental trauma can have an underdeveloped brain, which leads not only to learning disabilities but to problems with motor skills as well. Nadya's profile indicated that she was severely delayed in many respects, but as with Delaney, we wanted to draw our own conclusions.

First, we spent time sitting in a small circle and rolling a ball between the three of us. She seemed excited to play and had no problems with the ball. Karl and I gave each other a silent, hopeful look. At the same time, the orphanage representatives were observing us and taking their own notes, making sure we were a good fit for Nadya. All of them were pleasant and supportive, giving us nods and smiles of encouragement as we played with her. Only her social worker seemed stern, watching us with narrow eyes and pursed lips. She was more formally dressed than the others, in a collared shirt layered over a black turtleneck, black and gray hair cropped just above her shoulders, and low, thick bangs.

"She's sloppy and doesn't pay attention in school," she said matter-of-factly through our translator, looking directly at Nadya when she spoke. "She doesn't care about her grades at all," she added with a shrug.

Next, we wrote some English words on the chalkboard and asked Nadya if she could write them—which she did in flawless cursive handwriting.

"See," Karl said to me with a satisfied smile after she finished her third English word on the board. "She doesn't have a problem with not being smart enough." We thought her attentiveness and efforts with us on the chalkboard proved her social worker wrong. We were expecting

Nadya to have some form of ADHD; we thought that was to be expected for a child who had lived her whole life in an orphanage, and assumed that was the reason behind her poor academic performance.

Waves of relief and hope welled up in me—maybe Nadya *did* just need someone to pay attention to her in a positive way. She didn't speak much, but seemed shy—not obviously mentally disabled. We got the impression that the descriptions we had received of her underdevelopment were exaggerated, and our hearts swelled with love for her. Through our translator, we were able to have basic conversations with her. She would answer questions such as what her favorite dessert was (ice cream), and she asked if we could bring her some tomorrow (we did).

After the high emotions of that first day, we collapsed on our bed when we got back to the hotel, each of us quiet and lost in our own thoughts.

"All she needs is a family and love," Karl said as we both stared at the ceiling, taking in all that we had experienced.

I turned to look at him. While I was buoyed by that first day, I was under no impression that the hard part was over. "She doesn't even know the concept of 'family,'" I told him. "She calls us Mama and Papa, but she doesn't know what that is. She doesn't even know the meaning of love."

Especially for older children who have experienced abandonment, trauma, and life experiences that we can never fully understand, love can only heal so much. I was aware that we didn't know the extent of her issues after that first brief meeting. Karl's eyes closed and he finally fell asleep. I lay there going over all I had seen that day, wondering if Nadya was doing the same. Eventually I, too, fell asleep.

The next day, the orphanage director, along with our translator, took us for Nadya's dental checkup. The director was smiling and telling me how much Nadya looked like me; I thought that was very kind.

There was a small medical office in part of the orphanage, and a group of children were lined up on little chairs outside the room; they did not look excited to be there. The director let Nadya go first. I had asked if I could be present for the exam as I had previously worked as a dental assistant, and she agreed. I had looked inside Nadya's mouth the previous day and concluded that she had two painful abscesses and a few other cavities. Not surprising, since no children at the orphanage owned a toothbrush, nor did they know how to use one. I had packed a toothbrush for her and would show her how to use it.

A man in a white lab coat and very tall white hat motioned Nadya in and told her to sit on an older-model dental chair that didn't even recline. The translator and I stood off to one side. To my dismay, the dentist stood behind her and brought her chin up to look at him. She was crying and not happy to comply, and I didn't blame her. I went over to hold her hand, and that seemed to calm her. He took one look in her mouth and declared, "No cavities." That was the extent of her dental care, and I was too dumbstruck to protest. I realized I didn't want her to get any dental care there anyway—we just needed to get her to the US as soon as possible.

Those three days passed quickly, and we had spent barely four hours with her before it was time to say goodbye and head home. She didn't understand why we were leaving without her, but we told her we would be back in a month. She seemed despondent—crying and clinging to our legs as we said goodbye, no matter what reassurances we gave.

Again, Russian bureaucracy delayed our paperwork approval, and it was four months before we found ourselves on a plane to Siberia for the second time. This time, we brought Delaney and Connor, then aged seven and eleven. Delaney packed her suitcase full of toys and gifts to share, and Connor was ready to do research for the report about Russia he had to write for school during his time away.

After three days of traveling, including a night in Kemerovo and the two-hour drive to the orphanage, our family finally arrived on its doorstep. Delaney bounced up and down, and Connor's smile lit up the room as we walked in the door. The staff took us immediately to the room where Nadya was waiting, and Delaney ran up to Nadya and gave her a hug. Although Delaney was two years younger, she was about three inches taller than Nadya. They started giggling, and Delaney took Nadya by the hands as they jumped up and down with excitement. Nadya again wrapped herself around my legs, and I felt a tremendous surge of love for our new daughter. I was so glad to be reunited with her.

We had two hours together as a family. Connor brought a simple puzzle that he pulled out of his backpack and showed Nadya, inviting her to sit down at the table and work with him on it. Delaney had a Hello Kitty purse that was full of tubes of ChapStick, and she gave several to Nadya. The girls picked up some lion and bear hand puppets from the small toy bin in the room and began playing, making animal growls and putting on an impromptu show for us.

As we got up to leave, the girls skipped down the hallway toward us holding hands, and we were surprised that Nadya knew how to skip. It was one of the most beautiful moments in my daughters' relationship. *Maybe this is going to work out after all*, I thought. I don't know how I would have reacted if I had known then, as I know now, that those scenes would never again be repeated.

The very next day, we had our court date in Kemerovo to finalize the adoption. Just before we walked into the appointment, the adoption agency representative handed us an updated profile for Nadya. It was the first time we saw a document mention that she was aggressive—that she bit and kicked other children and caretakers. We were puzzled as to why we were only receiving this now, but we pushed it to the back of our minds, telling ourselves she did what she had to do to survive in the orphanage. Within an hour, the judge approved our adoption and Nadya was legally our daughter.

We arrived in the orphanage to pick her up on our third day. We brought her a new set of clothes—jeans, a warm sweatshirt, and a knee-length mint-green coat with a white fur-trimmed hood, along with winter boots, mittens, and a hat to protect her against the chilly March air in Siberia. She was officially ours, and her excitement and joy were palpable. She beamed from ear to ear as she opened the presents and looked at us wide-eyed and breathless, taking it all in. She had never had clothes of her own before, and she couldn't get them on fast enough! I helped her get changed and I thought that even though she'd never heard of Disney, she must feel like Cinderella going to the ball as we bundled her up to leave. Delaney and Connor giggled and bounced with energy, hugging Nadya a dozen times before she got her coat on.

She made the rounds to say goodbye to her caretakers and friends. As before, there were children scrubbing windows, walls, and floors. They stopped to look at us with sad eyes as we walked by, and Nadya gave hugs to a few of them. Her eyes were lit up, and she was full of pride at her new family; she couldn't stop smiling. I didn't want to look at the other children's faces, but I was drawn to them. I wished I could do something—take them all home. But I knew I would never see any of them again.

Outside the doorway, a little boy stood waiting to say goodbye to Nadya. She exchanged a few words with him and gave him a hug. He looked so forlorn standing at the top of the stairs by himself that I gave him a hug, too. He barely moved while our van pulled away. The gate closed behind us as several children ran outside to see us off, clutching the metal bars with tiny mittened hands as we smiled and waved. It was heartbreaking to see their small, smudged faces pressed against the gate. My body ached to mother each and every one of them—to wrap them up in my arms, comfort and rock them to sleep the way every child deserved to be rocked. My throat was dry and the heaviness of wanting so desperately to care for all these orphaned children made it difficult to take a breath.

As the smokestacks disappeared from view, Delaney started singing, as she often did. One of her favorites was a song called "Blessed Be Your Name," which we sang in church every Sunday.

Blessed be the name of the Lord
Blessed be Thy glorious name

Delaney sang the refrain a few times, and then to our surprise, Nadya joined in. Those were the first words we heard her speak in English. It was uncanny how easily she mimicked the sounds, even though she had no idea what she was saying. The drive back to the hotel in Kemerovo was full of singing and laughter, and Karl and I exchanged smiles of gratitude and relief as we observed our new family together.

. . .

A few days later, we were in Moscow finalizing Nadya's visa for entry into the US, and Nadya's senses were completely overwhelmed by the sights and sounds of the big city. Her head spun in every direction, and she stopped constantly to inspect cars, storefronts, and people that caught her eye. Her excited behavior bordered on manic. When we stopped in a store on our way back to the hotel, we could barely restrain her. She sprinted up and down the narrow aisles in a blind frenzy, pushing a shopping cart and running into people and shelves without even pausing to notice what she was doing. Delaney and Connor thought it was funny, but Karl and I struggled to get her out of the store without causing any real damage. Our hearts raced over how this might be connected to our little girl's overall personality, but we didn't stop long enough to think about it. We couldn't.

We then stopped at a restaurant for lunch—Nadya's first experience at a restaurant—and she continued to exhibit odd behavior. The only thing that got her to sit still was to pour one sugar packet after another into her mouth, which, of course, only made the situation worse.

We also noticed how difficult it was for her to transition between tasks—a hallmark symptom of children with various kinds of developmental trauma. She would freeze in front of every watch or jewelry shop, staring at the sparkling items, pressing her face against the glass. She wouldn't listen or come when we called her, and would stand there for a long time staring, while we all waited. I got my first glimpse of Nadya's "mean eyes"— the cold stare with narrowed eyes that made her look angry and hateful—when I insisted she come along with us.

"She's like a blind person who can suddenly see," I remarked to Karl as we watched her take in the stimulation with a mixture of apprehension and curiosity. She would look at us when we called her but then look away again, detached. She wanted to touch everything, including every car we walked past, getting her hands filthy and becoming defiant—looking me in the eye with a cold stare—when I told her not to do that. She refused to wear her seatbelt, which nearly gave me a heart attack when our driver drove up onto the curbs to bypass people or cars, which is not uncommon in Moscow. I didn't want to push Nadya too hard on anything from the start, so Karl and I mostly sat back and observed, while Delaney stared, wide-eyed, and Connor clung to his teddy bear.

In Red Square, the girls and Connor held hands and posed for pictures. *This is nice*, I thought in calmer moments. It seemed as though Nadya liked Delaney and that they might develop a good sisterly relationship. Those early days were full of hope.

That night in our Moscow apartment, Nadya sat on a wheeled office chair and aggressively pushed herself from one side of the room to another, as though on a roller coaster ride. She slammed into a wall, and a vase on the bookshelf crashed to the ground, startling me to my feet.

"Oh, no, Nadya, you have to stop!" I told her in Russian, but she wouldn't listen. She spun herself round and round on the chair, as fast as she could go.

"Please, Nadya, stop playing with the chair. It's not a toy." I tried to connect to her, but she ignored me and continued to spin, again pushing herself from one side of the room to the other. She fell off the chair but seemed to barely notice the impact, getting right back on to continue her wild playing. I told myself she was just excited. Eventually she did calm down, and I helped her change into new pajamas. I laid her down on the bed and went to change. When I returned, I saw she had found a purple marker on the desk and was scribbling in large lines all over the sheets.

"Nadya, no," I carefully scolded. I tried to keep my voice calm as I took the marker out of her hands. She stared at me blankly as I explained that we had to be respectful of property that wasn't ours. She didn't understand; all she knew was that I was taking something away from her and she did not like it.

I lay down in between Delaney and Nadya on the bed, while Connor and Karl slept on the futon in the living room. My nervousness had been increasing throughout the day as Nadya's behavior escalated. By bedtime, my insides quaked uncontrollably. *This is it*, I thought. *She is ours; we have to make this work.* Nadya lay perfectly still, staring at me for most of the night with questioning eyes . . . eyes that said, *Who are you? What are you doing with me?*

Delaney fell asleep peacefully, and I gazed at the ceiling as tears of anxiety and foreboding clouded my vision. I turned back to Nadya, who continued to stare at me, motionless and unblinking.

"I love you, Nadya," I whispered. "I am your momma." Despite the visible tension in Nadya's tiny body, I tried to reassure her that everything was going to be okay, stroking her hair for some time before she finally laid her head down and fell asleep.

CHAPTER 4
A BRIEF HONEYMOON

"Logan? Hi, it's Mom." I called my oldest son from the car. "Can you please make sure the dog is locked in the bedroom? We're almost home." My brother Bryan and his daughter from Milwaukee had stayed at our house while we picked up Nadya, both to watch Logan and to welcome us home with our new daughter. After nearly twenty hours of traveling and a long drive through scorched Texas earth, we were pulling into our driveway.

Hung on our garage was a Welcome Home sign my brother made. *It's nice to be home*, I thought. Nadya was quiet and withdrawn. I watched her intense, rigid stare at the unfamiliar landscape outside the window. She had wet her pants on the plane without making a sound. I was always asking her in my limited Russian if she was hungry, thirsty, or if she needed to pee—but besides taking a few nibbles of food, she never showed any signs of understanding what I was saying. I had helped her change in the airplane bathroom, and put a blanket down over the soaked seat. She didn't seem upset in the slightest, and even reached overhead to turn on the fan so she could hold her pants up to dry off. *That's strange,*

I thought. *She can work a fan on a plane but can't tell me she needs to pee?* I didn't know what to expect next.

We had shown Nadya pictures of our dog, Zoe, at the orphanage—but as with everything, it was hard to say if she really understood. She saw cats around the orphanage but no dogs. She was already so overwhelmed that I was afraid we were getting close to her breaking point. We knew it was best for her to come home to a quiet house, and not to introduce her to extended family until she was ready, despite how much they may have wanted to pinch her cheeks and shower her with gifts. We needed to work on bonding with her first.

From the driveway, Nadya timidly inched her way towards the house.

"Welcome home, guys!" Bryan beamed from the doorway. He crouched down in front of his new niece. "Hi, Nadya!"

She looked at him blankly as he gave Connor and Delaney a big hug.

We deposited our suitcases in the living room, and Nadya cautiously looked around. Gone was the excited little girl who wrapped herself around my legs and called me "Mama." She heard barking from Zoe, our elderly, hairless Chinese Crested, and angled her head in the direction of the sound. I held my breath as I indicated it was okay for Logan to let Zoe out. As Zoe ran towards us, Nadya swooped down and picked her up, squeezing the animal tightly to her chest.

Zoe was uncomfortable and squirming, scratching and trying to greet us, but Nadya had an iron grip. She seemed oblivious to the scratches on her arms and the dog's yelps. Zoe wriggled from her clutches and jumped up, panting heavily, to see us.

"Do you want to see your room?" I asked Nadya. The girls would be sharing a bedroom, with matching twin beds and pink comforters Delaney had picked out. Delaney was already halfway up the stairs, gesturing for Nadya to follow. Nadya looked up at Delaney, and by her tentative stance at the base of the stairs, I imagined she had probably never seen carpeted stairs before. I gently guided her as she held on to the handrail with both hands and took the steps slowly, one at a time.

Delaney ran into the bedroom and was bouncing up and down on her bed when we reached the top. Nadya stopped in the doorway.

"This one is yours." I pointed to her bed with an encouraging smile. She stared straight ahead, perhaps confused, scared even, as the corners of her eyes pinched slightly. I wondered what was going on in her head. I had recently purchased a large pink Barbie house at a rummage sale for the girls to play in, and Delaney ran inside and held up her toys for Nadya to see. We finally coaxed her into the room, and she stood in front of the bed. Everything was made for a little girl: pinks, delicate lavenders, and flowers. The room was strange to her, as I knew it would be. Delaney ran over and handed her a Barbie doll.

"Let's play!" she said.

Nadya glanced at the doll and put it down on the bed.

"Do you like your room?" I asked her. She looked at me blankly for a moment, and then suddenly crouched down and crawled under the bed. She pushed herself as far back as she could go against the wall.

My heart sank. *She must be so terrified and confused.*

I knelt down next to her for the next twenty minutes, but I couldn't coax her out—she just stared at me with wide, unblinking blue eyes, and Delaney played with the dolls by herself.

Nadya finally emerged as I was putting food down on the table about an hour later. I felt relief that she at least listened to her hunger and felt safe enough to join us for a meal. I knew the textures and smells—and just about every other detail—of what she was experiencing were completely different from anything she had ever known. She smelled everything before she put it into her mouth. If she didn't like the smell, she would take the food off her fork.

Every motherly instinct in my body ached to wrap her in comfort; to take away her fear.

"We have your favorite dessert, Nadya," I told her. "Ice cream."

The smile across her face lifted my spirits just enough.

• • •

The first two weeks at home were a cautious calm—the honeymoon phase. We tried to limit her exposure to stimulants like new people and outings so she could work on her comfort and bonding with us. She barely uttered a single word in those first few weeks, in Russian or in English. One day I found her balled up in the corner of her closet, crying. I knew that she would go through a grieving period once it sank in that her life in Russia, the only life she had ever known, was now gone. I also knew that this would increase her anxiety and possible aggression. She didn't respond to my comfort. She gave me a cautious look when I tried to put my arms around her; there was nothing I could do to console her. All I could do was sit near her. I felt so sorry for her. A new country, a new family, a house that was nothing like the orphanage . . . even the size of it when compared to the orphanage was different. There were no long hallways, no kids yelling or laughing, pushing or swearing.

My other children continued to try to engage her, and were generally confused by her actions. Delaney didn't understand why Nadya wouldn't engage in imaginative play with her—hadn't they played with puppets in the orphanage? Where had that gone? Was it all a show? At dinner, sometimes Nadya would laugh when we laughed, even though she probably didn't understand what we were saying. Karl made funny faces, and she responded to humor. Connor would sit at the table with her after dinner and play simple card-matching games that tested your memory. She participated and seemed to enjoy that. We were surprised at how well she remembered those cards. They also worked on puzzles together, and laughed while watching *SpongeBob SquarePants*. There were so many signs of hope.

Karl and I decided to get her a bike with training wheels so she could ride with Delaney, and to our great relief, she loved it. In fact, she loved it so much she refused to get off. I would walk around the neighborhood with her, Nadya zooming to and fro, and Delaney laughing and riding alongside her. Sometimes Nadya would pull into people's driveways and sit there right in front of their door. At first I didn't want to push her so I just waited her out, but it became problematic when she refused to move for twenty minutes or longer. Delaney had already gone home and put her bike away.

"Come on Nadya, let's go," I said with increasing urgency. "It's getting dark. We have to go home." *Home*, I repeated again in Russian. She stared at me. I walked up to her and took hold of the handlebars, starting to pull her bike in the direction of our house. She started yelling, kicking her legs, and swiping at my hands. I let go and stepped back, my heart racing. *Oh no*, I thought. *What is happening here?*

"It's okay, honey. It's time to go home." I hoped she would follow now when I started walking. She didn't. She continued to yell and kick, sitting on her bike. *I can't leave her here like this.* I took hold of the handlebars again and pulled her towards the house, angry now, not letting go despite her increased thrashing. She kicked and screamed as I pulled her down the sidewalk. Neighbors turned to look at the commotion, and Karl was outside the house when I pulled her up the driveway. He picked her up and brought her in the house, where she finally calmed down after we gave her some ice cream, but I was shaken.

She had been home for over a month now, but we still had not heard her speak a complete sentence in English. Every day I tried to teach her a few words from books and other materials. I would point at things, and she would repeat them, but that was the extent of her progress. She never said things on her own; she only mimicked me when I spoke. Her method of communicating consisted mostly of pointing and grunting. And her favorite word was *no*.

When we'd lived in Las Vegas the year before, I had hosted children from Russia as part of my work with the adoption agency. In the summer program, children eligible for adoption would visit with potential adoptive families in the US. In my experience, at the end of three weeks, a child the same age as Nadya would be speaking relatively coherent English, using complete, if simple, sentences. But not so with Nadya.

For the first few weeks, I stayed home with her to bond and didn't put her in school. About a month in, I took a part-time job at a daycare center down the street because our family of six needed two incomes now more than ever, even though I wished I could dedicate all of my time to developing a close, connected relationship with Nadya. We enrolled her in the local elementary school. Although she should have been in fifth grade, she fit in physically with the second graders. The administrators had no idea what else to do with her and put her in the lower grade.

The school had zero special education capacity for a child such as Nadya—not even ESL classes. She was going through the motions of her day, being herded from one room to another, all with no idea what was going on. Some days she just put her head down on her desk and slept. I felt helpless once I realized there were no resources at the school that could help us break through to our daughter, and I didn't know where to turn. We had educated ourselves as best as we could about the issues that arise when adopting older children, but looking back on it now, we were in the dark about the uphill battle Nadya was facing. She was obviously terrified, and we would learn later that all the kids in the orphanage had told her that American families kill adopted children to harvest their organs.

One of the Russian chaperones from the hosting program the year before had asked us about this very thing.

I nearly choked on my dinner! Despite all the outrageously sarcastic responses I felt like defaulting to in the face of such a question, I realized it had come from a serious place, so I answered it simply: No. We love them. We give them the opportunities that they would never ever have if they aged out of an orphanage. We give them stability that they never knew. We give them love that they have never experienced, and most of all, we give them hope.

One weekend afternoon, Nadya was out riding her bike, and I had to pull her back to the house again, kicking and screaming.

"Shhhh, please stop yelling, Nadya," I pleaded with her. "It's time for lunch. Aren't you hungry?"

When we got home, she ran into the backyard and paced back and forth. I didn't like her back there because there were mounds of fire ants she could stumble into, but there wasn't much I could do to stop her.

"Nadya, your food is ready, honey," I told her, gesturing for her to come inside. She gave me a cold, evil stare. I realized I was not going to get anywhere with her. *Oh well, she'll come in when she gets hungry*, I thought. I was frustrated and felt like I had a two-year-old instead of a nine-year-old. I turned to open the sliding glass door and go back inside. Without warning, Nadya kicked me— hard. I turned around, shocked. Connor and Delaney were sitting just inside the door at the kitchen table, and they scooted their chairs back in fear.

"That did not feel good!" I scolded her, knowing the edge of anger was clearly perceptible in my voice. I tried to calm down as best I could, taking hold of her arm and pulling her inside the house.

At once, she started screaming at the top of her lungs.

It was a scream unlike any we had heard—piercing and fierce. It was a gale-force wind that consumed everything in its path, and its immediate effect was to knock the breath out of me. Fear crawled up my skin, and all the hairs on my arms and neck stood up. I was frozen but knew I had to take control of the situation. I tried to explain to the other kids that she did not know better, that it would be okay . . . even though I knew it would not be okay. Not by a long shot.

Nadya ran into the living room and started throwing anything she could get her hands on. Pillows, pencils, remote controls—everything went flying. Zoe was barking and snapping at her ankles, and Nadya gave her a hard kick, catapulting her to the corner, where she yelped as she collapsed in a heap.

"Logan, take Zoe to your room!" I ordered, and he did his best to calm the small animal as she cowered away from the chaos.

We all watched as Nadya ran to the fireplace, grabbed a framed picture of herself off the mantel, and threw it to the ground, followed by every other photo on the mantel. I realized that I was witnessing a true rage for the first time. She was trying to break things that she knew had meaning to me. I could feel her erupting, her emotions surging in the room like lava on a path of destruction. I was at a loss as she stood in the middle of the living room and screamed at the top of her lungs. She paused only to refill her lungs, then continued shrieking. Not a single tear fell.

I was trembling and couldn't breathe. My heart pounded and my head ached. Everything was moving so fast; I wanted my kids to be safe. I wanted to protect them. And I didn't want them to see this.

"Why is she doing that?" asked Connor, then twelve years old, in a panic. Delaney stood behind him in the hallway, sheer terror on her face as the screaming and crashing raged on beyond us. I couldn't think straight.

"Connor, take Delaney over to David's house and hang out for a while. I'll let you know when things settle down. I'll be all right."

The kids were afraid to come down the stairs to where Nadya was, as they didn't know how to get past her or if she would attack them. They quietly snuck down the hall, avoiding her attention. She was completely focused on me anyway, and I turned to face this tiny whirlwind of rage wreaking havoc in my living room.

The barking, the screaming, and the crying became too much—I thought I was going to lose it. Logan, then seventeen years old, stepped out of his bedroom to check on the situation. He shook his head, wondering out loud, "Why the hell did we adopt her if we knew she had issues?" I didn't want to admit to him that that question had crossed my mind many times as well—I didn't want to admit it to myself.

He called out to me. "Ma, are you all right?"

"I don't know!" I called back.

He came down the stairs and tried to help by talking to Nadya in a quiet voice, but his efforts fell on deaf ears. Nadya was blind with rage.

"Nadya, honey," I started again. "It's okay, you don't have to scream." She looked at me with hatred. *What did I do?* I thought. My whole body shook as I tried to hold it together, tried not to freak out.

I went to the kitchen and showed her the sandwich

I had made for her. I pointed to the other children's half-eaten sandwiches on the kitchen table, and her untouched one next to them.

"Aren't you hungry?" I asked in Russian, gesturing to the plate, but she was beyond all reason. I realized she had become furious with me when I turned away from her in the backyard to come inside. She wanted my attention. She wanted to be in control.

Well, she was certainly calling the shots now. *What else can I do? Of course I have to pay attention to her, but I need to be the one in control. I need to teach her how to control her anger, but how?* She was not like our other children. What I was seeing was not the child we had met in the orphanage.

I knew Karl would be leaving work soon, and I silently prayed he would hurry.

"It's okay, honey," I said, as I approached, though I was shaking like a leaf.

She stood in the corner of the living room, hands in fists, body tense. She looked more like a cornered wild animal than a tiny nine-year-old girl—her body was consumed with a primal fight-or-flight response. I feared her the same way I feared an angry dog, and I approached with extreme caution. *If I try to hold her, she might calm down*, I thought. As she stood in the middle of our living room, yelling, I crouched down to put my arms around her.

And without missing a beat, she slammed her head into mine in a violent head-butt. I reeled from the sharp impact to my forehead as I released her. *Oh my God*, I thought, my head throbbing. How the heck had that not hurt her? I was truly starting to panic. Did she not feel pain? Perhaps in that state of heightened anger, she didn't. She didn't cry; only I was crying.

"Stop it, Nadya," I said to her sharply, trying a different angle. "Just stop it right now!" I yelled over her, hoping the firmness of my voice would snap her out of it. Nadya didn't let up for even a minute. *How do her lungs have so much power?*

I told Nadya if she ate her lunch, she could have ice cream afterwards, but nothing I said seemed to register. I knew she must be hungry, but here we were, locked in this battle, cautiously circling each other. I decided to sit on the couch and turn my eyes away from her. Maybe she would stop.

I continued watching her in my peripheral vision. She seemed most intent on hurting me, on throwing things at me. It seemed that she would rather see me dead than lose control, and that scared the hell out of me. A deep fear started to take root in my heart—how was I going to survive this? I did not want Logan to get involved; it might intensify the situation. But just his being there made me feel safe—this was a level of fear I had never experienced.

I realized I had to physically stop her. I came up behind her, wrapped both arms around her shoulders, shifted my weight onto one foot, and with the other swept her feet out from under her and gently brought her to the ground with me in a judo takedown I had learned in a martial arts class a decade before. *Never thought I would have to use this on my own children*, I thought. She was on her back now, and I quickly got on my knees, straddled her midsection, and held her upper arms and shoulders down while she thrashed. She was kicking so hard I could barely keep my legs in place, and she was trying to bite my arms. I was terrified, my mind frozen. *Please, Karl, get home soon. Please, God, please.* I had Logan call Karl to see where he was and how long it would take for him to get home. In the background, Karl could hear all of the commotion, and Logan tried to explain that he just needed to come home as quickly as he could.

Meanwhile, Nadya was snapping her teeth, covered in sweat. I could feel the heat and rage radiating from her. She had been screaming for almost two hours now and was showing no signs of letting up.

"If you stop screaming, Nadya, I'll take my hands off you." She looked at me in a moment of silence, her face red. I released her shoulders and moved to the side so I was no longer straddling her as she lay there. In a split second, she was up and screaming again, swinging wildly at me, trying to punch me, and running around the living room grabbing whatever she could get her hands on.

Logan tried to help. "Nadya, it's okay. Sit down. Want to go outside?"

She didn't respond.

This continued for the next hour—pinning her down, hoping she was calm, letting her go, starting all over again.

I had studied so much about the psychology of adoption, and yet I didn't know what was happening with her. I knew she was suffering from the communication breakdown, and also grieving the loss of all she had known up until then, but this kind of anger was way outside the realm of what I thought I understood. *I don't know how much longer I can do this; please, Karl, get home soon.* Finally, I heard the garage door open, and a moment later Karl hurried in.

"Oh my God, what is going on here?" he shouted as soon as he saw me from the doorway. He hadn't realized how bad it was until he saw me on the floor, pinning down this little out-of-control girl.

"Are you all right, Lori?" he shouted across the room at me.

Tears streamed down my face as I looked up at him from my position on the floor. No, I wasn't all right; I hadn't been all right for hours.

"I'm freaking out, Karl, freaking out," I choked out between sobs, trying to be heard over her screams. "Please, you have to take over for me."

He threw his keys down and ran over as Nadya jumped up, screaming. Karl grabbed her and held her down; his presence seemed to settle her a little bit. She got up, hot and sweaty, and hid behind one of our big living room recliners. Again like a threatened wild animal, she crouched down and stayed there, intent upon hiding.

I tried to collect myself. *God help me. God help me.*

Karl took me aside, away from her, and hugged me. "Lori, I am so sorry. What happened?" He looked from the hallway into the living room at the shattered pictures of our family.

I couldn't answer him—the truth was that I had no idea exactly what had sent her into this rage. What I did know was that I had to try to reconnect with her right now, but it was the absolute last thing I wanted to do. My nerves were frayed. I was shaking. I was afraid to get back in the game with her, so I spoke to her from a distance; I sat in a chair on the other side of the room and asked her to come out. I used what Russian words I knew. I didn't know how to engage her.

"Take a break," he urged. "You've had enough. We have to do something else with her. Go lie down."

Nadya didn't come out for another hour, when we were sitting down for dinner. She joined us at the table and ate her food, though the tension from earlier wouldn't dissipate. I went to bed shaking and crying that night, totally drained. Karl and I held each other in bed and prayed until we fell asleep.

CHAPTER 5
LIVING IN FEAR

A few days after Nadya's first rage, the girls and I sat in our Dodge Durango waiting for Logan to get out of school. In the rearview mirror, I caught a glimpse of Nadya and Delaney laughing while they played a silly hand game, and I felt the tension in my shoulders ease, just slightly. The memory of Nadya's screaming was starting to fade, and I smiled to think that maybe they could be like real sisters. Maybe her rage that day was just a fluke. I was looking for Logan when suddenly I heard a loud slap from the back seat. I turned around to realize that Nadya had slapped Delaney full force across the face. Delaney was stunned, her cheek pale with impact and quickly turning red.

"Nadya!" I yelled, as Delaney started to cry. "Stop that!" My adrenaline skyrocketed as my motherly instincts took over. *Oh my God, you hit my daughter*, I thought, horrified. *But you are my daughter.* I couldn't wrap my brain around it. Delaney cried and screamed, and Nadya responded in kind—flailing and kicking the seat in front of her.

"Get in the back of the car," I yelled at Delaney, urging her to get out of her seat and scrabble into the third row.

I was terrified Nadya would hit her again. At that moment, I saw Logan walking up and I motioned for him to get in the backseat. He opened the door and heard two screaming girls. I could tell the scene our family was making embarrassed him, and he quickly got in beside Nadya.

"Whoa there, Nadya," he said, trying to calm her. "Easy, it's okay. No need to scream."

She wasn't registering anything Logan or I said, and Delaney cried in shock and pain in the back row. Nadya turned her kicking to the car window and swung her arms at Logan, refusing to put on her seatbelt. Once again, she was wild, and I thought the window would break under the force of her ferocious kicks. I was thankful that we had parental safety locks on the doors, or else she could open the door while I was driving. *Please, God, just let us get home in one piece.* It was a ten-minute drive, and I don't know how I made it home in that panicked state. I drove in a rushed haze, hunched over and barely breathing, frantically scanning the rearview, my mouth dry, conscious of the chaos unfolding behind me. Delaney ran out of the car and over to her friend's house as soon as I parked, and Logan helped me get Nadya inside.

Logan was afraid of her as well. "She's crazy, Ma," he shouted over her screams. She was quick and fought dirty, as we soon found out.

She kept raging once we got inside, but after about an hour I was able to coax her out of it with ice cream. It felt like a devil's deal, but I needed the moment of reprieve. When I went to pick Delaney up from her friend's house, I had to explain to the other parents why her cheek was so red. I was mortified. I don't think any of those parents understood we had adopted a disabled child, and I was met with curious and even suspicious looks. I had no idea what to do or how to talk to Nadya to prevent this kind of thing from happening again.

A week later, we were leaving the daycare center, where the girls' school bus dropped them off, and they piled into Karl's pickup truck. The backseat, which is much smaller than the one in the Durango, seemed to shrink even more when I heard Nadya screech.

"Delaney!" My heart jumped into my throat.

"I'm sorry I stepped on your foot," Delaney said quickly, a frightened look on her face. She looked at me for help. She was already expecting Nadya to explode, and I could see the anger rising in Nadya's eyes; in her mind, nothing was an accident—*everything* was on purpose.

"It's okay, Nadya, honey," I said quickly, hoping to avoid the meltdown. "Delaney didn't mean to do that. It was an accident."

Nadya yelled and grunted as they sat down, kicking the backseat, going from quiet to raging in an instant.

"Mommy," Delaney pled. "Mommy, I'm scared. Make her stop."

"Shhh, it's okay honey. Just climb up here in the front seat by me."

As Delaney moved forward to maneuver her body over the center console, Nadya grabbed her by the shoulders and pushed her back into the seat.

I turned and shoved Nadya back down in her seat.

"Sit down!" I firmly told Nadya. "Now, Delaney, get up here!"

Delaney scrambled into the front seat, cowering into the door as she cried.

This made Nadya even more furious, as she doubled down on the tempo of punching and kicking the back of the passenger seat where Delaney sat. The force of her kicking was pushing Delaney forward, hurting her even through the seat. I quickly put the car in drive. As I sped down the side streets, something sharp and heavy made contact with the top of my head. I slammed on the brakes and turned around to see Nadya retract her arm as she prepared to whip my head again with a set of jumper cables she'd found lying on the floor. Her arms heaved forward, swinging the cables with all her tiny, rage-filled might. Delaney's hand hovered on the door handle, ready to launch out of the car.

"Nadya, stop it!" I yelled, as I tried to duck the thick cables. "Sit down," I barked. "And put your seatbelt on!"

Nadya screamed, and I covered the back of my head with one arm as I crouched forward, trying to drive with my free hand to get us home and get both Delaney and me out of the path of Nadya's rage.

Oh, please, God, don't let us die in a car accident right now. Please.

"Just keep your head down!" I shouted at Delaney. "Stay down!" It was the longest five-minute drive of my life and I was on autopilot—crying and terrified.

On Nadya's next swing, I managed to grab the cables and hold on to them with one hand, driving with the other. She struggled to pull them away from me. We were locked in a frantic tug of war until we pulled into our driveway and Delaney and I both jumped out of the car.

Nadya continued to scream and kick and wave the cables around. Karl heard the commotion and ran outside, his face strained with worry. Delaney immediately ran, crying, to her daddy and threw her arms around him.

"Delaney, we will take care of her. Go to David's house," I said. This was beginning to be a pattern that I didn't like.

Karl swooped in to help me with Nadya. She kicked and bit at him like a snapping turtle, and I was horrified as I watched this sometimes-sweet little girl turn into something from a horror film.

To restrain her, we dragged her out of the backseat and straddled her torso on the kitchen floor, holding her shoulders down—it was the only way to prevent her from hitting or biting us. In the one moment Karl let go, she was up in a flash, tearing into the living room like a tornado. She grabbed to the picture of us that hung over the fireplace and chucked it with all her might onto the ground. She ran down the hallway and started opening and slamming the doors to the bedroom and bathroom, over and over again—and she would continue doing this for hours.

We sat upstairs in the loft, waiting for the storm to fade. Connor was in his room trying to do his homework.

"Make her stop banging the stupid doors already, will you?" he begged.

But there was nothing we could do. She ran around the house like a wild animal, and Karl and I took turns subduing her—with force, when necessary—for hours, until her rage passed. By the next week, Karl had taken all the doors off their hinges, so we had to use the bathroom with the door open.

Our lives were unraveling before our eyes.

Later that night, Delaney and I stood quietly near the

kitchen sink and whispered. "I'm scared of her," she admitted.

My heart felt broken. The truth was, I was scared of her, too. I was scared that I would drive off the road and kill us all while Nadya raged in the backseat. I was scared that my family would spiral into a long, dark abyss that would end in misery and chaos. I was scared we had already done irreparable damage to our other children, and I had to promise Delaney that Nadya would never hit her again. I prayed I would be able to keep that promise.

Soon, rages of this caliber happened daily, and we knew we needed help. Within a few days of the jumper cable incident, we decided to check Nadya into the hospital for a psychiatric evaluation. We packed her bags and told her we were going on a little ride. When we pulled up to a local hospital, Nadya was immediately confused and scared—she knew this was some kind of institution, and I knew it would remind her of the orphanage, but we needed help and I hoped an evaluation, some answers, and possibly some medication would give us much-needed direction.

We met with a doctor and sat in his office, while Nadya crouched with her knees up to her chin and her arms wrapped around her legs. Karl and I battled mixed emotions. Should we keep her here? Should we take her home? She cried and looked at us as if we were giving up on her, abandoning her. It took us eleven hours to finally decide to have her stay for the evaluation.

We escorted her to the room where she would be staying, outfitted with two single beds made up of thin, hard mattresses on cold metal frames. There was a simple, worn, square table in between them with a small lamp, and the walls were bare and dull white. It was sparse and scary. I had to remind myself that this was temporary, and she would get evaluated, get on some meds, and come back home. Karl and I stood in the doorway as she sat down on the bed. She looked at me and pointed at the other bed.

"Sit down," she demanded. *Don't leave me*, said her pleading eyes.

I looked at my poor little girl sitting alone in this sterile room, and I sucked in a breath that I intended to steady my words. "I can't. But I promise we'll come visit you tomorrow." It felt as though my insides were being ripped apart. I swallowed back my tears.

"This is for your own good," I said. "These people are going to help you feel better. We'll come back and get you soon," I promised. But she wouldn't look at me; she wouldn't let me touch her. She just sat there, staring at the other bed, crying and alone.

"Oh, God, Karl, are we doing the right thing?" I sobbed into his shoulder as he supported me down the brightly lit maze of hallways and out to the car. My whole body hurt from the sadness.

"She needs some medicine, Lori," he assured me, his voice quiet and steady. "This is the right thing to do."

That night, I cried for hours into my pillow, thinking about her all alone in that hollow room, frightened and shaking and feeling abandoned. It was a strange feeling to realize that I missed her, but we suddenly had peace and calm in the house, and I desperately wished we could keep it.

Please, God, just let her fall asleep easily and quickly, I prayed. *Please let her know we did not abandon her.*

And then I fell asleep.

We were up early and drove to the hospital in the serene June morning, both of us quiet and lost in our thoughts. As the psychiatrist called us into the consultation room, I noticed the dark circles under Karl's eyes, and I knew mine looked the same.

I rushed in, hungry for information. "How is she? Did she sleep?"

"Nadya is fine," he said matter-of-factly. "She is just finishing breakfast in her room, and you'll be able to see her soon.

"The issue right now," he continued, "is that your daughter is at a point where the brain-based internal controls for modulating emotion are often compromised, resulting in her becoming easily overwhelmed and struggling to return to a rational state. A psychopharmacological intervention, such as an initial course of psychotropic medication, would be warranted."

They had put her on an ADHD medicine, as well as Valium and a mood stabilizer.

"She also has some sort of attachment issue from her years in the orphanage," he added. "We don't really specialize in that area, but I think it's a severe form of what we call reactive attachment disorder, or RAD." He went on to explain that it was caused by sustained abuse or neglect at a young age. His voice seemed cold and clinical, and my stomach tightened as he explained his conclusions.

That would explain her severe symptoms, I thought to myself, feeling short of breath as it sunk in that she had much higher special needs than even we had anticipated.

The social worker we met with next was more to the point.

"I have been a social worker for twenty-one years in the state of Texas," she began. "There are more suicides that happen because of the lack of mental health care in our state than almost anywhere else. We have a brand-new state-of-the-art children's hospital with no behavioral clinic. Pack your bags and go back home to Wisconsin. You are not going to get help here."

We were shocked by this advice—we had barely arrived in Texas, Karl had a good job, and we enjoyed the warm weather. I couldn't imagine uprooting our family yet again and moving back to a place we had tried for so long to leave. I felt numb.

After those meetings, we visited with Nadya, who seemed listless and detached when we entered her room.

"Home?" she asked, looking up at me with pleading eyes.

"No, honey, I'm so sorry," I said to her, my voice breaking. "The doctors need to keep you here for a few more days to make sure you're okay. We'll come back and visit you tomorrow," I said, but again she wouldn't look at me.

Karl—my incredible, patient anchor—was as confused as I was, but we never gave up on loving her. That night, we held each other in bed and cried. We had conflicting emotions—and guilt on top of guilt that regretting her adoption could even cross our minds.

"This is all my fault," Karl started. "I got us into this, I pushed for the adoption." He sat slumped on the edge of the bed with his head in his hands.

"That's not true. Don't blame yourself," I said. "We both wanted her . . . we both knew we wanted to be the family for Nadya."

"Even after you warned me about the dangers, I pushed

for it," he said and paused. "I should have listened to you."

"Don't say that, Karl," I pleaded. "We both love Nadya. She was brought to us for a reason."

"I'm so sorry for her—so sorry for the life she was handed as an infant," he said. He wanted so badly to make everything right for her.

"You realize that there is so much 'wrong' with her, we may not ever get it right," I said as tears ran down my cheeks. "We may not be able to heal her."

"I know," he said. "I know. That's what I'm so worried about."

These were the very things I had foreseen from the beginning. Our family was fractured, but would we be normal again? In the dark, I prayed to God for enough strength and wisdom to parent—and love—this little girl.

A few days later, Nadya returned home, but it was clear that even with the medication, there was no improvement. I didn't understand how it was possible, but the Ritalin, Valium, and mood stabilizers only made her sleepy. Her anger showed no signs of abating. She raged daily—usually when she had to transition between tasks. I walked into the kitchen after one particularly long episode of Nadya's screaming, and saw Karl standing at the counter, pale and shell-shocked. I noticed his face was thinner than normal, his skin dry and papery. I was barely eating and did not know how on earth I was still doing my adoption job with all of the stress and chaos at home . . . but somehow I was. I was bringing families together while, ironically, mine was being ripped apart.

"We have to take her back to the hospital," Karl said. "There's got to be something they can do for her."

Neither of us was prepared for the severity of it all;

how can anyone really be prepared? It's impossible to accurately imagine how helpless, torn, frustrated, fearful, and angry you might feel in the scope of such a life-changing situation . . . and we were painfully aware of how the adoption was affecting our other children, how terrified they were.

As we drove home after checking Nadya in for another weeklong stay, I hated admitting to myself that everyone felt better when she wasn't in the house. We were laughing again. Delaney could snuggle with Karl and me. She could be the baby of the family once again.

I had to fight to not let myself slip into a very dark period—which I knew was especially important for my other children. I knew how much they were being affected, and I tried to maintain a strong front for them. I desperately tried to function in my old state of familiar normalcy. *What have I done to my children, to my family?* I thought on days when I was overwhelmed with guilt, just barely clinging to the threads of reality as I remembered how wonderful our life had been before Nadya. I missed the sound of Delaney giggling with her friends in her room, and the ease with which we used to have family dinners full of jokes and teasing every night.

The only thing that kept me grounded was the solid bond and relationship I had with Karl. We completely supported each other through this grueling period. The fact that we had any reserves at all with which to approach our traumatized daughter was because we were always on the same side—always loving and supporting each other.

In the meantime, I also immersed myself in research about RAD and international adoptions, and found a resource that gave me great hope—the International Adoption Clinic, part of the Children's Hospital of Wisconsin.

"Karl, look at this," I said excitedly to him one night while Nadya was still in the hospital. "This is not far from where we used to live, and they have specialists in international adoptions and attachment disorders." It was obvious to us that this was where we needed to go. Karl and I saw a light in the distance, and I pinned my hope on it.

In late August, barely four months after we'd brought Nadya home, we packed the last of our things in our car and started the long drive from Texas to Wisconsin. I stared out the window as we drove through the Texas flatlands for the last time, embarking on a journey of desperation and hope. We had moved to Austin with such great expectations for our family, and were leaving bitterly disappointed by how little support we had found. *How I wish I had known this before we adopted*, I couldn't help thinking. I daydreamed of peace, quiet, and a life where help for my family was not a four-letter word. I prayed we were heading in the right direction.

At this point, all I could do was pray.

CHAPTER 6
DESPERATE FOR HELP

We had arrived within arm's reach of the help we needed, but to our dismay there was a six-month waitlist for an appointment at the International Adoption Clinic (IAC). We might as well have still been in Texas. The only option for care we saw at that point was to enroll Nadya in a regular elementary school and get the school's support by having them implement an Individualized Education Program (IEP), which is mandated by the Individuals with Disabilities Education Act (IDEA). An IEP is put in place by a team of educators and caretakers to set educational goals for a child, and is the basis for developing a framework to help educate a child who would flounder in a regular classroom setting. Nadya had a disability diagnosis from the psychiatrist in Texas, and we were hoping it would mean the school would dedicate individualized resources to her, such as a one-on-one aide, speech therapy, and certain behavioral supports, at a minimum.

The school's psychologist did an informal evaluation of Nadya—a futile endeavor as Nadya would barely engage with us, let alone a stranger. Unsurprisingly, the results showed she understood and spoke English at a two-year-old level, essentially understanding only a few isolated words; her memory skills were in the low to low-average range. Her cognitive scores ranged low to low-average; she had difficulty recognizing patterns, understanding relationships, and engaging in abstract categorical thinking. It was not encouraging, but we also knew that her silence throughout most of the exam (whether in silent opposition or to mask confusion) made assessing her "true" functioning an art form at best.

One morning in mid-September, Karl, Nadya, and I headed to the school to meet with Nadya's team. We hoped to get some answers on what they could do for our daughter, though I knew Nadya wouldn't understand much of what was talked about besides her name.

We sat down in a conference room with the school principal, psychologist, social worker, special education director for the school district, and Nadya's homeroom teacher to review records and test results and to discuss Nadya's future at the school. Nadya had refused to get dressed when I asked that morning, either locking herself in the bathroom or screaming at me. Running late, my nerves were frayed and I knew dark circles ringed my eyes.

I looked to the team assembled at the table with us for guidance.

"Thank you so much for coming," started the principal. "We've reviewed her records and gone over her test results, and well . . ." He faltered. "We're not exactly sure what the best course of action is. We've never had a child quite like Nadya."

"To put it simply, we think Nadya's main issue is that she doesn't speak English," said the school psychologist.

"We think she needs ESL classes first and foremost."

"Her not speaking English is not the issue," Karl and I both started in at the same time, surprised at his assessment.

"We've been trying to teach her English for almost half a year now, and we're not making progress," I said. "She needs more individualized attention at school, and counseling or therapy—something. Something to teach her how to handle anger, and make her feel safe and comfortable. Only *then* will she start being able to learn anything."

It was as if they didn't hear me.

"Our school social worker, psychologist, and the special education director agree that the best thing at this time is to put Nadya in ESL classes," said the principal. "This will be through regular education, every morning for two hours. We'll assess her progress and the situation after she's been enrolled for some time."

"No, no," I started in, panic rising in my chest. "You're not understanding me. She has experienced complex developmental trauma because of what happened to her before we adopted her, and she needs to work with someone who understands the issues related to that." I had been doing my reading and I knew that children like Nadya often experienced repeated exposure to trauma, which included things such as extremely poor care, severe abuse, or neglect, in early life. As a result, they suffered not only from symptoms of RAD, but also ADHD, post-traumatic stress disorder (PTSD), and various behavioral disorders—all of which could be combined under an umbrella of "complex developmental trauma."

"We appreciate that," said the psychologist. "But we

think if we can get her to communicate properly first, it will alleviate a lot of the issues. Oftentimes we see that communication problems are the underlying cause of behavioral and emotional problems. It's actually quite common in children with autism."

"That's not what she needs," I said, flummoxed. "She needs speech therapy *and* one-on-one attention."

The entire team sitting across the table proceeded to tell us that since she spoke Russian at home, English was her second language so ESL classes were warranted.

"We do *not* speak Russian at home," Karl replied firmly. "We have only been speaking English since we adopted her, so if she were capable of learning English easily, she would have done so by now. Russian is her native language, but she does not speak it at all! As we have been trying to tell all of you, we do not speak it, *she* does not speak it—we have only heard her say a handful of Russian words in all the time we've known her. She has trouble communicating in any language. You, of *all* people, should understand ESL, and this is not an ESL case."

"I've been studying with her every day," I added. "She is not just going to start speaking English because you put her in an ESL class. That is not the issue," I implored them from across the table. The group of faculty members shifted, noticeably uncomfortable, and looked at one another.

"We believe you," started in Nadya's homeroom teacher. "But we just don't know what else to do for her right now."

What I didn't have the clinical words for at the time, but which I understood intuitively as a mother and as someone who worked in the adoption field, was that Nadya's brain had trouble acquiring *any* language. What

I wished I had known then was how to explain to them that Nadya had probably missed the important window in early childhood when her brain needed to wire itself for speaking. If a child has not been spoken to and encouraged to speak during this critical time period, the necessary neural connections never develop, often resulting in lifelong delays related to language and communication. I was sure that Nadya's brain had spent most of its time in her early years wiring itself for fight, flight, or freeze—which was adaptive at the time, but left her handicapped when it came to other skills necessary for relating, communicating, and thinking.

Sadly, Karl and I were on our own, with just our instincts and no one to help us advocate for our little girl.

"She needs to be evaluated for an IEP," said Karl. "She needs individualized attention for issues other than just her language."

"Well, to be perfectly honest," said the principal, "she's actually not entitled to an IEP."

"What?" I answered, almost not comprehending what I was hearing. "Of course she is—according to the report from the psychiatrist in Texas, she is emotionally and cognitively disabled."

"Oh, we know that, and believe me, we *really* want to help," he continued. "But actually the state of Wisconsin requires that a child be a US citizen for three years before they become eligible for an IEP."

We were stunned. The law was geared towards children who immigrate with their entire families, and is in place to prevent spending resources for an IEP where basic ESL classes would be enough. We did not feel the law applied to us. We thought the school was hiding behind it to avoid spending the money to get Nadya the resources she needed.

"That can't be," said Karl, sounding dazed. "We've just moved our entire family across the country to try to find help for our little girl, we're on a six-month waitlist at the International Adoption Clinic, and now you're saying you won't help, either?"

The nightmare seemed to darken the room around me, and I wiped the palms of my hands against my thighs.

"We know she has needs, and we are going to do our best to accommodate her," said the principal, "but again, we're just not sure what to do with her right now." They looked at us sympathetically, but we felt completely hung out to dry, as though there were nothing we could do or say to clarify our needs. In short, they had never dealt with a child like Nadya, and were totally unprepared.

"You can't just put her in a regular classroom," I pled, nearly begging by now. "She will make no progress. She needs to have a special education teacher to help her read and write. She will get nowhere otherwise."

"We know she needs more attention than the average child," said Nadya's teacher. "But our hands are tied right now because of Wisconsin state law."

They can't help our daughter; they don't know what to do with her. These were supposed to be people I could count on to educate my child. How could the systems designed to help children and families in this country be so hard to access?

The principal handed us a pamphlet that described the ESL program. We were confused but believed what they were telling us—that there was nothing they could do for three years. I felt intimidated and didn't know how to respond; we assumed their word was final. I walked out of the meeting holding Nadya's hand and gripping the damp, crumpled, useless pamphlet in the other.

Nadya entered the second grade—again—and went through the motions of her day. The school did assign her classroom helpers who would take her to and from lunch and recess, or who would open her folder to the proper page the class was working on. But she didn't do any work and didn't speak to anybody. Delaney felt sorry for her and sometimes tried to play with her during recess, but mostly Nadya was alone, watching everyone else. The other children could not communicate with her at all, and they soon gave up trying. She was physically in the school during the day, but mentally and emotion-ally, she was gaining nothing from it.

The one blessing throughout all of this was that Nadya wasn't violent at school—if she had been, they surely would not have allowed her to stay. She wasn't violent toward Delaney, either. All of her anger seemed directed at me.

Not every day ended in a complete rage, though, and I started keeping a list of the positive days—the times when she came home without me having to physically drag her, the times she sat down to dinner and ate her food without yelling. She never readily listened, but her refusals took place on a spectrum. She was really never cheerful or happy, but when she grudgingly did what I asked, I uttered a silent prayer of thanks. She looked forward to when my brother Bryan came to visit from Madison, and she enjoyed sitting and drawing with him. He made her smile because he was always cracking jokes and making funny faces.

In the meantime, while we waited for Nadya's intake for outpatient therapy within the IAC, I went to the library and checked out every book I could on attachment disorders, and did online research as well. Most of my reading gave me clinical definitions and explanations, but none gave me practical advice or suggestions on how to connect with my daughter.

One night, I lay in bed reading *The Connected Child*.

"Oh my gosh, Karl," I sat up suddenly, excited. "You have to read this." This book was a godsend. For the first time, I heard some specific guidance on how to handle transitions and mitigate Nadya's morning rages, since they seemed to happen then most often. Through *The Connected Child* and other resources I found at the library, I started gaining more insight into how to understand the effect of trauma on my daughter's brain.

Experts believe the human brain is only about 25 percent developed at birth; the rest of the neural connections we need in life are made after birth and are based largely on experience. The most used connections become strongest, while the least used fade away. When a child is constantly under stress in his or her early life, the neural connections for the stress response—namely, the fight or flight reflex—can become hardwired in a child's brain. This kind of chronic stress, which can result from severe neglect (such as being left alone in a soiled diaper for long periods of time, or never being picked up or comforted), can disrupt early brain development. This explained a lot of why Nadya was cognitively delayed, and it helped me to understand that in order for her to get better, she needed to rewire her brain and build healthy, new connections in a safe and comforting environment. Everything I was learning gave me a sense of hope. I wasn't giving up on her, despite how hard it was—and how much harder it would get.

Most mornings I could barely drag myself out of bed, walking the stretch of hallway to the girls' room like I was walking the plank. Daily, and this morning was no exception, I approached their door with a painful, tight knot in my stomach, not knowing whether it would be Jekyll or Hyde on the other side. My fear consumed me. There were hardly any words to accurately describe how terrorized I felt.

I stood outside their bedroom with my hand on the doorknob, closed my eyes, and took a deep breath. *God, give me strength, please*, I prayed. *Please.*

"Good morning, girls," I said in the most cheerful voice I could muster. I could tell what kind of morning it was going to be if Nadya turned to me with an evil, hateful look, and then turned away again. In those moments, my heart sank, knowing it was going to be a long, drawn-out fight. This day, however, she rolled over to face me, and while she certainly wasn't cheerful, she was looking at me, which I took to be a positive sign.

I gave Delaney a good morning kiss, and she got up and started getting ready.

"Good morning, Nadya." I sat down on Nadya's bed, stroking her hair.

She didn't reply.

"Ready to get started on your day?"

Again, she looked at me blankly.

"Okay, here we go," I said gently. "Remember these?" I pulled out a photo album I had created. It included a series of pictures that I had taken of Nadya successfully going through the steps in her morning routine. It started with a picture of her in bed with her pajamas on, which is where I always greeted her in the morning. Then there was a picture in the bathroom—Nadya sitting on the toilet, pointing to the toilet paper. Next was a picture at the sink, washing her hands. Each step of her getting dressed was a picture—starting with a picture of her underwear, then her shirt, then her pants. Everything had to be in order. A picture of her pills, then a picture of her taking her pills. Sitting down to breakfast. Separate pictures for putting on her boots, then coat, then hat. A picture of her in the driveway, and then standing at the bus stop, and even one of her standing on the stairs of the bus.

I went through these pictures with her every day. For every one she completed, she could pick out a couple of M&Ms from a bag I carried, enjoying the candy on the bus to school. Dr. Purvis's book had given me the idea. *Okay, maybe there are some tools that will help me make progress.* But almost as soon as the thought came, Nadya lost interest in the candy and the pictures, and wouldn't engage me in the mornings. It was back to being one big fight.

In the larger scheme of things, it was difficult to make progress amidst the rages. When she raged and screamed all night, it was incredibly difficult to wake up in the morning and start all over. I felt as if I were at war, constantly looking out for—and often stepping squarely on—land mines. Any brief success was mitigated by a larger sense of floundering. And we felt that we were losing our other children, too. They all stayed away from home as much as possible, never had friends over anymore, and tiptoed carefully around the house when they were home. Gone was the laughter, noise, and pleasant tumult that came with having three active, healthy children. Our house was now either uncomfortable silence or wretched screaming.

One morning, I reached such a point of panicked overwhelm that I made a desperate phone call I'd hoped I would never have to make.

"Greenfield Police Department," said the operator. "What is your emergency?" I held my hands over my head to protect myself from Nadya's punches.

"I have a daughter with reactive attachment disorder, she is adopted from Russia, and she is being violent and biting and kicking," I cried in one fast breath, Nadya screaming all the while. "She's out of control!" I yelped in desperation. "She's hurting me! Please send someone! I need help."

I knew the operator could hear the screaming.

"Are you hurt, ma'am?"

"Yes, but not badly, she's only nine. You need to send someone," I pled, sobbing, as I cowered in the corner of the hallway just outside the girls' room.

"Is anyone else in the house with you? Is anyone else hurt?"

Out of the corner of my eye, I saw Delaney, fully dressed for school but her face awash with fear. I could hear her whimpering, "Not again, not again." Connor had already gone to school and Logan to work.

"My youngest daughter is here, but she's not hurt," I said as I tried to focus on Delaney through my tears. The terror on her face almost destroyed me as she watched me trying to shield myself from Nadya's kicks and punches.

A few minutes later when the police arrived, Delaney

scrambled downstairs to let them in. Nadya paused at the noise they made walking in, the loud beeping of their walkie-talkies and their authoritative presence commanding the space. Two police officers stood at the top of the stairs and tried coaxing her, but they got no response. I ran downstairs and frantically wrapped my arms around Delaney, who was also crying.

"Shh, it's okay," I whispered into her sweet-smelling brown hair. "Shh, the police are here now. It's going to be okay," I said, trying to mask my uncertainty.

"Mommy, I'm so scared," she cried. "I don't want to leave you."

"It's okay, honey," I soothed, wiping the wetness off my cheeks. "The nice policemen are here now and they're going to help us."

She gripped me tightly and my body shook with emotion as I hugged my scared little girl.

"Shhh, it's okay," I said. "I know that was scary for you to see. I promise I'm going to be okay. Hurry, I hear your bus coming." I gave her a kiss and told her to go down the driveway to wait. Nadya would not let me go outside with Delaney, so I told Delaney I would check on her in school when things calmed down. I could see all the kids had their faces plastered to the windows at the commotion and flashing lights in front of our house. Delaney tried to hide her tears; I could tell she was embarrassed by all the attention her sister had caused.

Nadya eyed the officers like a feral animal.

"It seems she's settled down, ma'am," one of the officers said to me. "What would you like us to do?"

Uncertain, I took a deep breath and shrugged my shoulders. "Would you mind just staying for a little bit to make sure we're going to be okay?" My voice trembled. "I need to call my husband." I was trying to speak, but the lump in my throat strangled me. I needed water.

"It's okay, Nadya, right?" I turned to her. "Are we going to be okay now? Would you like to have a drink of water?"

Nadya ran and hid behind a chair in her room. The policemen eyed the scratches and bruises on my arms.

"What would you like us to do here?" the officer asked. "It looks like you've been abused. We could take her down to the county hospital?" he said, referring to the Milwaukee County Behavioral Health Division.

The thought was absurd to me.

"She's not abusing me," I replied. "She has no idea what she is doing." I knew what this must look like to outsiders, and it made me angry because it wasn't true.

The officer shrugged. "It's your call."

I could sense the rage dissipating, as Nadya was quiet and watchful. "It's okay, gentlemen," I said. "Thank you for coming. I think we'll be okay now." I walked them to the door feeling like I was moving through molasses. I knew I was anything but okay. I offered Nadya a drink of water, and she gulped it down and handed back the glass.

"It's okay, sweetie. We can start again. We can always start over. You're not bad. I love you." It took everything in me to say those words.

Going forward, I contemplated the darkest thoughts that had ever entered my mind, daily. *How can I end this? I can't take this anymore. I just want it to end.* I was horrified that the thought of taking my own life had started to cross my mind, but the thoughts came and went like specters, and I was helpless to do anything about it. It was my secret. I closed the bathroom door and slid down the back of it. I sobbed with my head between my knees, praying for help. *I have other babies, they need me. What the hell am I thinking?* I drew in a deep breath as other thoughts floated into my head. *Nadya needs me. Karl needs me.* I felt torn in more ways than I could imagine.

I wasn't sure who I was anymore. I was losing myself. I could not recognize myself in the mirror. I even practiced the smile I gave everyone so they would think I had it all together. My hands shook all the time, I could barely eat, and I couldn't remember the last time I had gotten any decent sleep.

My family was a mess, and I was hanging on by a fine string that could snap at any moment. I cried about how much I hated this little girl, how I hated what she had done to my family, but I knew I could never let my other children see me this way. I was in a tug of war, constantly back and forth, hating her and then loving her. I wondered if she had the same battle within her as well: loving me, then hating me. I knew that none of this was her fault . . . she didn't ask for this, she deserved to be loved, and she was my daughter, but how could I keep going in this way?

"We have to send her somewhere," Karl said to me one night. "We can't have our family ripped apart like this."

"But she *is* our family," I reminded him.

Our lives were a twisted version of *Groundhog Day*. I woke up, said a prayer for strength, thanked God for the day, and asked him to provide patience with Nadya and my other kids. And on we went.

CHAPTER 7
A DOWNWARD SPIRAL

In the spring of 2008, the big day arrived: we would finally meet with the International Adoption Clinic at the Children's Hospital of Wisconsin, which is affiliated with the Medical College of Wisconsin. I had anticipated this day for months. A few weeks earlier, we had sent in dozens of forms for the required paperwork, explaining as much as we could about Nadya's background and the issues we were facing. *These people will know what to do,* I thought as we walked into the bright lobby.

It turned out that at the time, the clinic focused on medical issues related to international adoption and had physicians who were specialists in that field, but they didn't have a psychologist on staff who specialized in adoption issues. After all this time, we still weren't going to get the specialized care we had been hoping for; we were devastated. Instead, we were referred to the regular psychiatry clinic for behavioral health, and Nadya started attending weekly sessions there. Since she wasn't very verbal, she and her therapist spent a lot of time drawing and engaging in play activities, while I waited outside. It didn't seem like much, but I was glad it was something.

While weekly therapy was a step in the right direction, Nadya continued to rage at home. Over the course of the next several months, I called 911 a handful more times, and usually it was the same two officers, a man and a woman, who responded. Gradually, they got to know Nadya, and sometimes instead of settling down when they walked in, the intensity of her rages increased.

"What's going on today, Mrs. Hetzel?" asked one of the officers when I let them inside.

"She won't take her pills; she needs to take her pills," I sobbed. As was the norm, by this time, my whole body shook with adrenaline. I was a mess.

The other officer took the pills from my hand and crouched down, offering them to Nadya on his open palm.

"Now, Nadya, you need to take your pills." His voice was stern.

To my amazement, she stopped screaming, picked them up, and put them in her mouth, curiously eyeing him.

"There you go, that's a good girl."

This medicine was to calm her rages—it was specifically designed to dissolve in her mouth within thirty seconds and was supposed to work immediately. We had used it several times and it never had any effect on her, but we hadn't stopped trying.

Nadya held the pill in her mouth for almost a minute, staring at the officer at eye level. I could sense her fuming anger.

"Good girl," he said.

With that, she spit a mouthful of half-dissolved pill into his face, once again screaming at a piercing volume. He used a loud voice and told her not to do that. For whatever reason, she was particularly worked up, and she ran to me, flailing at and punching me again, right in front of them. Those little fists were her weapons. The officer stepped in between us to stop her, and she immediately took a step back, staring at his imposing presence. Breathing quickly, she glared at me, her hands balled up. I swore I could hear my bones rattling.

Nadya's face was beet red as she spit and started to scream again. The officers must have thought she was possessed by the devil.

At one time, we did too.

The officer raised his voice, telling her to stop, and she ran and hid behind a chair. Through the commotion, I kept trying to explain to them how and why she became this way . . . but reactive attachment disorder is complex, and given the current situation, it didn't come out as clearly as I would have hoped.

The same officer who was spat on came near me. "Ma'am, we can't leave you like this."

The female officer tried to talk to Nadya in a friendly voice, attempting to keep her away from me, but Nadya continued to run, scream, throw things, and slam doors for what felt like hours but must have only been thirty minutes.

Eventually, Nadya locked herself in the bathroom and continued wailing. The officers stood at the bathroom door and tried to talk her out of it. They took turns telling Nadya that she needed to stop what she was doing, but she would not respond. They tried to reassure her that everything would be okay, but there was no reasoning at this point, even though they were genuinely kind to her as they tried to settle her down.

Then, the more familiar officer glanced down to notice the bite mark Nadya had left on my arm earlier that morning; it was already dark purple and swollen. I was grateful she hadn't broken the skin.

He sighed and shook his head. "We're going to have to call the paramedics. She is out of control, and it is unsafe for both of you."

I felt numb and paralyzed as I looked at broken candles and remote controls, the holes in the walls, and the upended chairs. I looked wearily back at the officer, whom I knew was only doing his job. I barely nodded my assent. Nadya came out of the bathroom and sat on the front room chair with fear in her eyes, grabbing her legs and shaking.

Oh, my God, oh my God, I thought. *This is my life. This is what I go through every day.*

The paramedics were at our door within minutes.

It took a team of four EMTs to get hold of Nadya and strap her to the board. She screamed and cried as they strapped her in, her previous rage compounding and turning into terror.

"No, Mama, no!" she cried, reaching out to me as they restrained her arms under the straps. "Please, no! I will go to school! I will go to school. Please no, Mama!" It was rare to hear Nadya speak a full sentence, even a short one. I knew she was desperate.

"Shhh, it's okay, honey," I managed to say as I let the paramedics work. "I will be right behind you," I said, choking back tears.

"Mama, Mama, Mama, Mama," she cried in succession.

When they closed one of the back doors to the ambulance, her wails and screams were only barely muffled.

The paramedic turned to me and said, "We're taking her to the Milwaukee County Behavioral Health Complex."

I grimaced. I didn't want her in another institution. What's more, it was an older complex that was harsh to look at on both the inside and out. I was skeptical but desperate.

I nodded and peeked through the one open ambulance door. "I am right behind you, baby. I'm coming. I will be right behind you."

I was heartbroken; despite all my best efforts, this was it. I had no idea what else I could do for this little girl. I called Karl and he met me at the hospital—yet another day he needed to take off from work.

In some ways, the county psychiatric hospital felt like we were back in Texas. The feeling that we had to institutionalize our daughter—again—tore us up inside. The same things we'd done in Texas—like check her in and communicate to administration through a bulletproof window with a hole the size of a grapefruit—made us deeply uneasy, but we were at the end of our already frayed rope.

It seemed to take forever to go over insurance, and I had to have Karl talk while Nadya sat with me, looking around tearfully, telling me she wanted to go home.

We walked with a nurse to find Nadya an available bed. The place was loud and crowded, and Nadya kept looking up at me with sad eyes, knowing that we would be leaving her here.

What was worse than the guilt I felt was that I hated it here, too. I didn't want my daughter to be here. It was full of so many troubled kids, and I worried about her safety. There was nothing that made this place any friendlier than the other places she'd stayed. There was nothing cheerful that would ease her mind, not one picture to look at or kind orderly to brighten her day.

They suggested keeping Nadya for a week, but we couldn't leave her there that long—the place was too scary, even for us. Plus, Karl's insurance would be changing the next day, and we would be eligible to check Nadya into an inpatient psychiatric hospital—the Dewey Center at the Aurora Psychiatric Hospital—that her psychologist had recommended. We knew we could check Nadya in there on an emergency basis for a weeklong stay, despite their six-month wait list for the day-therapy program. So, after one day in the county hospital, we had Nadya moved directly to the Dewey Center.

The Dewey Center was night and day from any inpatient experience we had had so far. They were familiar with RAD, and it was a simple blessing not to feel judged for having an out-of-control child. Nonetheless, as with every other short-term hospital stay, there was little they could do for Nadya. They evaluated her, upped the dosage on her medications, tried to engage her in therapy, and then sent her home. The one good thing to come of her stay was a phone call I received a few weeks later.

"Hi, Mrs. Hetzel," said a voice on the other end of the line. "This is Linda with the Aurora Dewey Day Treatment program."

"Hi, Linda. How can I help you?" My curiosity was piqued.

"We have some good news for you. A family has dropped out of the day treatment program, so a spot has opened up. We moved Nadya up to the front of the line for admission."

I sat down at my kitchen table, speechless. We had been told it would be another three or four months before a spot opened up.

"I . . . what?" I stammered. "What are you saying?"

"We understand the severity of Nadya's case," Linda said. "We want to help your family and get her in here as soon as possible."

I was overwhelmed with gratitude, not only for our daughter, but also for our family. She would now attend a special day treatment program at the Dewey Center, surrounded by therapists who worked with special needs children. Unlike the inpatient psychiatric hospitalizations we had thus far experienced, where the focus was on immediate de-escalation and discharge after one to five nights in the hospital, a day treatment program would provide longer-term care while Nadya remained in our home. Day treatment included three hours of daily therapy (individual and group therapies), as well as increased observation and monitoring of the effects of her psychiatric medications. Enrollment in a typical day treatment program generally lasts four to six weeks. Though I didn't know it when Linda called, Nadya would end up participating for nine months.

For the first time in this whole ordeal, *real* hope surged through me. I was ecstatic at the thought that she would be getting focused, intense treatment every day—and I knew the rest of the family would share my sense of relief. I couldn't wait to tell Karl the good news.

CHAPTER 8
EXPLORING ALL OPTIONS

We enrolled Nadya in the Dewey Day Treatment Center with great hope and optimism. A small bus would pick her up every day, and to my great relief, the bus driver, Mr. Jenkins, wouldn't leave until Nadya was on board. On mornings when she was being especially difficult, he would shut off the engine and walk up to the house to try to coax her out.

"Hi, Nadya," said the large, jolly black man standing in our doorway. He grinned at her.

Nadya was often fuming silently in the hallway at this point, avoiding eye contact and ignoring anything any-body said to her—behavior our therapist at the Dewey Center termed "silent refusal."

"Don't you want to come to school today?" Mr. Jenkins asked sweetly. Nadya stared straight ahead at the wall.

"Come on, dear," he continued. "I'll let you sit up front with me." At that, she turned to look at him. "That sounds good, doesn't it? You like sitting in front, don't you?"

She didn't answer, but picked up her backpack and slowly followed him out.

"There you go, that's a good girl," he said as he gave me

a wink and walked back out to the bus with her.

"I love you, Nads!" I yelled after her. "Have a good day!"

She didn't turn around.

I breathed a sigh of relief, shut the door, and sank to the floor in a heap of emotion.

From the start, Nadya brought home daily goal sheets that I had to fill out with reports on her behavior. There were checkboxes for things like being helpful, following directions, taking her pills, and interacting nicely with others. She got mad if I didn't give her a good review and wrote honestly that she hadn't done well at home the night before—it would trigger a rage. She ripped the sheet in half sometimes because she didn't want to have to talk about her behavior in school that day. I eventually figured out that if I wrote a bad report, but then added smiley faces and exclamation points, Nadya would assume it was good because she couldn't read. On evenings when she was starting to get riled, I reminded her I would have to write down her behavior so Mr. Paul, her favorite therapist at Dewey, would see it the next day.

One night, our entire family was sitting at the kitchen table, ready to eat. Nadya paced just outside the kitchen.

"Nadya, I know you are trying super hard so that I can write down how great you're doing," I told her. "Please sit down with us and eat before your food gets cold."

"No! I don't want to sit next to *her*," she said, referring to Delaney, who rolled her eyes. Thanks to the specialized attention she was getting at Dewey, Nadya was becoming much more verbal.

"Then come over here—you can sit on my other side," I told her. "If you don't listen, I *will* have to write it down so therapy can help you."

"No, Mom," she said angrily, as I paused and waited for a reply. "I can do better," she added. We considered her admission of wrongdoing a major step in the right direction. She double-checked to make sure I wrote down that she apologized; she wanted Mr. Paul to know that she had self-corrected. I was so full of hope at these signs, though they were few and far between.

Nadya also started doing art therapy. This was a particularly good fit with Nadya as she continued to struggle with expressing herself verbally. In the therapy sessions at Dewey, the children worked on drawing pictures of themselves doing correct actions. Nadya drew simple scenes: one of her taking her pills in the morning, or one of her saying thank you with stick figures and a dialogue bubble. She couldn't write the words without help, but it was one of the only ways she could start internalizing the "right" behaviors she needed to learn.

A large portion of her treatment at the Dewey Center was participating in group therapy, which she hated. She didn't trust other kids, which I knew was a holdover from her years in the orphanage. Every day, she was encouraged to say just one sentence in group therapy—whether it was a comment about what she had for dinner the night before, or something that made her happy—and she would get a star for the day. She rarely communicated in sentences that were longer than five words, but we still thought this was progress when we saw her therapist's weekly reports.

As the first few weeks of her time at Dewey turned into months, we became anxious to see more changes in her behavior at home, because overall, there wasn't a significant shift in her rages. The silent refusals were just as hard on me, emotionally, because of the complete helplessness I felt. There was nothing I could do for this child except sit by her and wait (she would start to yell if I walked away). Her silent refusals were her way of maintaining control over the situation, and holding my attention prisoner. I struggled to remember that for Nadya, control meant survival, so she worked to control all aspects of her life, including my actions.

The psychiatrist in Texas had also diagnosed her with oppositional defiant disorder, or ODD, and while that *seemed* to describe her behavior, I knew she wasn't choosing behavior specifically to hurt or anger me. I knew that children with RAD exhibited oppositional behavior because they simply didn't know better. They didn't have the skills to exhibit the appropriate behavior to have their needs met. In the first nine years of her life, this behavior was adaptive, making up for the lack of routine, security, or care. As frustrated as I would get, seeing her as hurt, rather than oppositional, allowed me to connect with her vulnerability and maintain some level of calm in response to her behaviors. Remembering all of this made it hard to see this child as a malicious, vindictive being.

I often thought about how difficult it must be to live in that tiny body, always alive with turmoil and fright. She had adapted in her early childhood with the primal survival response of "fight, flight, or freeze"—and it was this pattern that she repeated; she didn't know how to do anything else. As difficult as she was for me to deal with, I knew she wasn't just "being difficult," the way a normal, healthy child could be when they "know better" and *choose* to disobey. Nadya didn't have the luxury of choosing her behavior—she didn't have the skills to do so, and she reacted in the only way she had ever known. Her behavior might have been appropriate in an orphanage or in a place where no one loved or cared about her, but it wasn't effective for us here and now. Her constant demands on my attention and her ability to fly into a rage at a moment's notice made me feel I was losing my mind.

At a certain point, we realized the only thing we could do was keep her safe and try to keep her from hurting others or herself. Occasionally, her violence still escalated beyond that and we were forced to call 911. The police were never a distant presence in our house.

As frightening as the physical aspects of her rages were, the emotional toll I felt was much worse. The frustration and helplessness would drive any sane person crazy. Over time, I realized that the constant emotional strain I felt was, in many ways, similar to how Nadya perceived the world. I had learned that some parents start to mirror the internal feelings of traumatized children, and I certainly started to feel traumatized myself. Even though I knew more than most adoptive parents because of my work within adoption agencies, it didn't take away the sting I felt from her hurtful behavior or the constant fear of its onset, even though I knew she wasn't being mean on purpose. I wanted so desperately to love her and hold her, but all I got in response was hateful looks that turned my heart to ice, breaking it a thousand times a day.

Still, I knew how important it was for us to keep working on our bond—it was the painfully slow process of teaching her about healthy attachment, and I did little things throughout the day to help her feel connected to me. Sometimes it was as simple as a paperclip. I would take two identical paperclips from my desk, and as I sent her off for the day, I would show her I was keeping one in my pocket that would remind me of her; she could do the same, I'd say. I told her that whenever she missed me or started to feel anxious or bad, she could just pull out that paperclip and know that I was thinking of her.

"When you come home from school, it will still be in my pocket," I assured her. She didn't say anything, but took the paperclip and silently put it in her pocket. Things were so tumultuous and physical with her almost daily, and I knew it was important that she realized that no matter what, I was not going to be pushed away from her. She needed to know that no matter how bad it got, I was in it for the long haul—that I wouldn't abandon her. I know I didn't always do the best job of maintaining that exterior, and sometimes it felt like a façade I was hiding behind. Nonetheless, I knew I had to regroup every morning, and try, try again. Recommitting each day to my practice of loving her harder was the only thing I could do.

We kept holding out hope that her daily therapy at the Dewey Center would translate into improvement at home, but change didn't come. It was certainly a great program for kids with many kinds of disabilities, but for Nadya, it wasn't enough, and her lack of improvement meant that I was becoming increasingly neglectful of my other children. I was going through the motions and making supper, trying to have what we called "lap time" with Delaney in the evenings, where I could just talk to her or read her a book, but usually Nadya's rages and moods made it impossible. Plus, Nadya was furious when I showed affection to my other children; it only made her behavior worse.

I tried to talk Nadya down as soon as I saw her clenching her fists and breathing hard. She would look around as usual to see what she could throw. I had to straddle her and hold her down, and I found myself yelling at the other children to go to their rooms, go outside, or leave the house. It wasn't fair. They deserved a mother, too, but I was pouring all of my energy into Nadya.

Delaney, in particular, suffered because she lost her place as the doted-on youngest child. I knew how hard it was for her to go to school when the police were at our house in the morning.

"Nadya was hitting again," she would have to explain about her older sister. The burden weighed on her, and that, too, broke my heart. In the mornings when she left for school, she tried to conceal her fear, but I knew she was scared to leave me because she was afraid Nadya would hurt me.

Logan, our oldest, remained distant, while Connor was more vocal. He hated constantly seeing me get hit, becoming defensive for me and furious at her.

"Stop it, Nadya!" he'd yell as she screeched and swung at me.

"Don't get involved," I would say. "Just stay out of it. Your two cents are not going to help."

Nothing anybody could say in these situations would help, but they could certainly make it worse. *Could it really have been just over two years ago that they were watching SpongeBob when we first brought Nadya home, playing card games at the table?* The memories were so distant that they now only appeared in glimpses at the edges of my weary mind.

I'm cheating my other children out of a mother, I thought. It was always in the darker moments when I found myself in deep sadness, contemplating how I got myself into this situation. It didn't take long before I developed a type of post-traumatic stress disorder; I felt like I was going to set off a land mine by just walking through my house. None of us ever knew what would set Nadya off. I was not the mother I wanted to be, yet I believed God had chosen me for Nadya for a reason, and I prayed and kept faith that everything would work out for the best in the end.

Also at this time, the school, our friends, and even our pastor seemed to judge us. (This was why we left our church; if your pastor cannot support you, who can?) Some perceived us as being "bad" parents, while others—after seeing how it was affecting our family—questioned us out loud for adopting a troubled child. The sense of isolation was overwhelming and painful. I barely got dressed each day and longed to get out of the house, but I had nobody to meet me for coffee and to just sit and have normal conversation. Everything revolved around Nadya and her behavior. I had nothing new to give my friends—nothing.

My best friend thought we were crazy for adopting an older child, and she let me know as much. She kept saying, "Look what you have done to your other kids, Lori. What are you going to do? This isn't fair to them. Can you give her up?" I got sick of hearing about how I screwed up. I wanted her to support me, but she could not. After almost twenty-five years of friendship, we just stopped calling each other, and I knew in my heart it was because of Nadya.

"She's just damaged goods," said another friend who was over at my house one afternoon and witnessed one of Nadya's screaming fits. *God doesn't make any junk*, I fumed. *A child is never junk*.

"It's not her fault what happened to her in Russia," I managed to respond, my defensive anger brewing inside. "She would just be discarded and kicked to the curb if we didn't help her, so that's what we are doing. Besides," I said after collecting myself, "she was God's child first before she was ever mine. I have to be her mother because she doesn't know what a mother is and every child deserves to know what a family is."

Despite my best efforts, I found that I was shaking all the time—the tremors that racked my body were constant reminders of how far this experience had worn my nervous system.

"You can't live like this," my brother said after he'd seen Nadya rage at something innocuous. *I know,* I thought. *But what can I do?* I had committed to caring for this child as her mother.

"You can't keep her," he added when he saw the struggle on my face.

"That's absurd, Bryan," I said.

"Can't you send her back to Russia?"

Here it is again, I thought. "No, I can't," I fumed through clenched teeth. "And even if I could, I *wouldn't*," I added defiantly. "Of course I know how it is, how it looks. But I just can't buy her a ticket and put her on a plane back to Russia. I am her mother. No matter what, I am in it for the long haul. She needs me."

He shook his head at the bruises on my arms. "You can't just let her beat you up like that every day. Look at you—you're a mess. You're my sister and I love you. It hurts me to see you this way."

I stared at him blankly; the truth was, I didn't know what to say anymore.

"I don't want to go to work and leave you here with her," he continued, his concern mounting.

Finally, I answered. "I'll be fine." I reached for the anti-anxiety pills that took the edge off just enough to let me make it through the rest of the day.

• • •

After nine months, the Dewey program ran its course and Nadya's treatment was over. While the program was hugely successful for other children, one year later we were back to square one—this time enrolling her in third grade in the local elementary school.

The school still refused to give her an IEP, so she received no special education. We argued with them about its importance but to no avail; at a certain point, we suspected they just didn't want to spend the money on acquiring the resources she would need—whether that was a specialized educator or even specialized education at another facility.

We contemplated hiring a lawyer, but the costs seemed daunting and we didn't know what we could do. We were the only advocates Nadya had, and we didn't know how to get her any help. As humans are known to do—as Nadya herself had done—we adapted, and our family reached a new normal of low-level chaos, fear, and stress all the time.

CHAPTER 9
DOCTOR WILSON

A year had passed, and Nadya's weekly therapy sessions in the psychiatry clinic didn't seem to be making much progress. She still wasn't as verbal as we hoped she would be by this point. The IAC notified us that they now had a psychologist on staff who was a specialist in international adoption issues, and advised us to have a consultation with her. *A specialist! Finally*, I thought.

I squeezed Karl's hand as we walked toward the beacon of hope on the day of our first appointment with her. A young, cheerful woman with medium brown hair and a warm smile held her office door open and invited us in. Our little family sat down in a small room full of colorful posters and toys.

"Hi, I'm Samantha Wilson." She reached out to shake both of our hands. She looked to Nadya. "Hi, Nadya," she said and then repeated it again in Russian. "You can call me Dr. Sami," she said gently, smiling a calm, broad smile and looking our daughter in the eyes for a moment.

"You speak Russian?" I asked, surprised.

"Just a few words," she explained.

Dr. Wilson informed us that she specialized in the

psychosocial development of children adopted interna-tionally, many of whom were from Russia.

I nodded, soothed.

She went on, with warmth and kindness in her voice, "I've reviewed all the materials you sent in. Thank you so much for doing that. It sounds like things have been hard for your family, and for you, Nadya. Tell me about it."

It was the first time in nearly three years that I felt like I was talking to someone who truly understood what our family was going through. Even in this initial consul-tation, I felt tears of relief well up in my eyes as I poured my heart out to her.

She nodded and took notes. Her training and special-ization not only supported children who developed in the context of neglect and trauma, but also hurting and sometimes hopeless parents.

Dr. Wilson set her pen down and looked up at us. "You have done many things to help Nadya feel safe within your family—that is fantastic. I know it has not been easy, but I can see your dedication and I want to help. But it might not be in the way you expect . . . *you* are Nadya's best therapists. I see my role as helping you discover ways to soothe her, find joy with her, and ultimately to share love and connection. So I ask you to join me in therapy so that together we might find ways to help Nadya heal from the hard experiences she has had."

It felt like pure oxygen was being pumped into my lungs for the first time in ages, and I felt energized at the hope she presented.

"One or both of you will always be here, and we will work on supporting your relationships with Nadya, seek-ing ways she can communicate her feelings and wants and exploring ways you can connect with and soothe her at home."

We started seeing Dr. Wilson weekly, and while she was a marvelous psychologist, it was slow progress. Karl and I were grateful that for the first time, we didn't feel alone. Most of the sessions were just trying to make Nadya comfortable. She would sit next to me and usually not look at Dr. Wilson directly for some time. We tried to play simple games together and make a social connection with each other. But much of the work was understanding my own reactions to Nadya.

One of the most important lessons Dr. Wilson taught me was that Nadya reacted first and foremost to my body language. The stance I took and the fear in my eyes often triggered her primal stress response (i.e., fight/flight)— the same way it would a cornered animal. For the first time, I was aware of how much my stress, fear, anxiety, and anger contributed to and maintained her rages. Dr. Wilson worked with me on how to recognize and regulate my own emotions so that I would be in a better position to control my physical posture. As she reminded me, "The powerful amygdala soothes the vulnerable amygdala," which was her way of reminding me that I needed to provide a calm, regulated presence before I could reduce Nadya's fight/flight response.

Parental power, she explained, came from calmness, not intimidation or reactivity. Nadya's brain had developed strong emotional patterns from the constant stress she was under in the orphanage, and I learned that words could have very little effect on a child who was guided by the frightened, emotional part of their brain. In times of behavioral crisis, I learned it was important to talk *less*, get physically *low*, and move *slowly* (if at all), all while trying to remain emotionally *neutral*. As I sustained my calm, eventually Nadya would start to mirror me and calm down herself. I used to completely distance myself from Nadya when she raged, and now I started to understand the importance of trying to maintain closeness (and calmness) with her, even the tiniest bit.

I also began to fully understand how my daughter's behavior was the only way she knew how to communicate with us. She didn't have the language skills in her brain to tell us how she was feeling; she didn't connect words to emotions. She was eleven years old, but had the verbal capacity of a three-year-old, just about the length of time she had been with us. Nadya couldn't tell us she was overwhelmed. She couldn't say, "I'm really scared when I go outside because all those noises feel overwhelming to me." But I could see that when I tried to get her out the door, she suddenly became rigid and then noncompliant. I learned that when I saw this coming, it was important for me to get lower and smaller than she was and that actually it was best not to talk. I needed to *show* Nadya physically that I was not a threat—that was the only way I could lower her stress response. If I simply told Nadya that she was safe but was hovering over her, her brain would still perceive me as a threat. Very slowly, with Dr. Wilson's help, we started to develop ways to give Nadya tools to communicate about her internal world with *language*, instead of behavior.

Karl and I were always involved in her therapy, which I now understood was a key component of healing for a child with attachment-related issues. Sometimes we would just do simple exercises where Nadya would hide behind the couch and build a Lego tower, telling Karl what she was doing so that he could build the same kind of tower. It was important for her to learn that she could communicate and be understood by others who have different perspectives.

Another therapeutic game we played was practicing being blindfolded and letting the other person feed us. I would go first, modeling behavior for Nadya that showed I was comfortable being vulnerable and that I trusted her to give me something safe and tasty to eat. Then we would work on her doing the same thing.

Dr. Wilson also taught me the importance of reconnecting with Nadya immediately after a behavioral episode ended. She explained that repair was vital to showing Nadya that we, as a family, could handle whatever pain she was experiencing and that relationships can endure.

"It's a learning process," Dr. Wilson reassured me in one of our sessions.

"I know. I just wish I had known half of this stuff before we brought her home."

"But you're learning it now, which is what matters," she said. "You know, this is really hard on her, too. I think it's even harder on the kids than it is on the parents."

"I believe that," I said, and it was true. No matter how much I felt I was falling apart, it was even harder on Nadya, who lived her own life in terror as well.

"I feel myself learning so much—I'm changing," I told Dr. Wilson.

"She will teach you, and you will teach her," said Dr. Wilson. "That's the best way therapy happens with hurt children."

. . .

In the fall of 2010 as Nadya entered fifth grade, and with Dr. Wilson's evaluations and recommendations, the school finally gave her an IEP based on her behavioral issues. She would finally be pulled out of regular classes for one-on-one education with a dedicated, trained special education teacher. However, even with Dr. Wilson's help, my mental state was so perilous that I had little hope for any real change.

By this point, almost every promise had failed us, and we'd lost confidence in whatever options we were presented with. Even though special education was what we had fought so hard for, we now felt it was too little, too late. It had been three and a half years since we had adopted Nadya, and we still felt that we had no idea what we were doing. And yet, despite feeling like leaves whirling about in a strong wind, we were willing to try anything.

CHAPTER 10
OUR LAST HOPE

My feet pounded against the soft grass as I ran through the yard, my heart racing in my chest. I hadn't run like this in a long time, not since I playfully chased Delaney around the house when she toddled around so many years ago. But this time I was running fast and in fear, looking for Nadya.

We lived in a mixed residential and commercial area. Our house was on a busy street, and only one small office complex separated us from a busy intersection, which is why, when I looked through the back window and realized Nadya was gone, my heart swelled into my throat faster than I knew what was happening. She was so naïve; it would be easy for someone to lure her into their car with as little as a picture of a puppy.

Most evenings, I watched Nadya through the kitchen window as she played outside in the backyard. Insects and animals fascinated her, and she examined the dirt—some of it loose and some of it hard-packed—to see what gems she could find. She collected ants, bugs, moths, and especially box elder bugs. Whether at home or at school, she would put them in her pockets, and I often found her with ants crawling down her pants by dinnertime. I had decided to only buy her jackets and pants without pockets.

Despite her visible connection to the earth, I was always cautious while she was out back. Even if I was just sitting at the kitchen table, I kept an eye on her at all times. The moment I realized I couldn't see her, I hastily slid the sliding glass door open and stepped outside.

"Nadya," I yelled, expecting her to emerge from behind a tree or between the bushes. "Nadya, where are you?" My heart beat harder as my mothering instincts kicked in. *Oh, my goodness,what if she's out in the street? What if someone has abducted her?* My nerves jangled as I tried to keep my panic at bay.

"Nadya! I have a treat for you," I yelled again, hoping she was just playing a game with me. I crossed the porch in three quick steps and strode down the two stairs, scanning the dusk for my daughter. I headed across the grass to the spot where I had last seen her, then toward the row of bushes at the far back corner of the yard, all the while yelling her name more and more urgently.

When it dawned on me that she was definitely *not* in the yard anymore, that's when I ran.

Although we had a large grassy yard lined with bushes, nothing was fenced in and I was always aware of the faint buzz of busy street noise one block away. It would be easy for Nadya to simply make her way between the bushes and find herself in the parking lot of the office building next door.

I scrambled forward, my eyes darting back and forth. She could have also become hyper-focused on a bug, following it wherever it went without regard for her surroundings. She could wander right into traffic chasing an insect.

"Nadya, where are you!"

Karl heard my yelling and came outside to join me. "What's going on?"

"She was just here a second ago," I answered, panicked. "I was washing the dishes at the window and I looked away for a minute and she was gone!"

We searched the perimeter of the yard, looking between all the bushes, hoping she was just silently refusing to listen to us and that we would find her digging in the dirt with a stick.

No such luck.

I ran up and down the outside of our yard, heading toward the busy street. My mouth was dry from the sense of frantic urgency as we ran to the street and back, not sure what to do.

In that moment, I noticed a police officer and a woman in the distance, walking down the street towards our house. Nadya walked alongside them, staring down at the sidewalk.

"Oh, Nadya!" I yelled. My dread was replaced with relief as I ran up and put my arms around her.

"We found her in the office complex next door, ma'am," said the officer.

"I saw her wandering around the parking lot by the bushes, and I asked her where she lived but she wouldn't answer me," said the woman. "I thought it was best to call the police." She explained she worked at a dental office in the small complex near our house, and hadn't seen where Nadya had come from.

"It wasn't until I arrived that she pointed to this house

when I asked her where she lived," said the officer. "So we thought we would just walk her right over."

All told, Nadya was gone maybe half an hour. Tears of relief filled my eyes as I held my daughter close to me. Her arms were limp at her sides, and she stared off into the distance.

"I'm so sorry, officer." I wiped my tears with the back of my hand. "I don't know how she got away. I was watching her play outside through the window, and then from one minute to the next, she was just gone."

"It happens sometimes," the officer said kindly. "Just try to be more careful. You might want to consider installing a fence." He gestured to the bushes, and I nodded. The thought had crossed my mind, but we were just renting and didn't plan on being there forever. Besides, I thought bleakly, even if we had a fence, she would find a way to get out.

"Nadya, you scared me so much!" I bent down to look at her. "Please don't do that again! Your dad and I were so worried about you. Nadya, do you understand?" I held her shoulders and looked into her eyes. "It was very dangerous for you to run away like that. Bad things could happen to you."

She nodded halfheartedly but refused to go inside the house. We all stood in front of the door and urged her inside, but she looked away and stayed silent.

"She does this sometimes," I explained to the officer and the woman. "She is cognitively delayed—she's not trying to be difficult." I heard the desperate plea in my own voice.

"Come on, Nadya, honey." I touched her shoulder, but she moved aside and refused to look at me. She didn't go in. *Please, Nadya, please,* I prayed. *Please just go in the house. Don't make any more of a scene.* But Nadya looked up at me with her "mean eyes," and my stomach sank. Those eyes had become the signal to the outside world that Nadya was unlikely to cooperate (perhaps aggressively so) with whatever request had been made of her.

The officer saw we were having difficulty and tried to help. He attempted to pick her up under her armpits, and she immediately burst into kicking and writhing.

"Whoa there, little girl!" Surprised, he turned to us. "Man, how much does she weigh?" He struggled with how difficult it was to hang on to her. I knew from experience that when she was flailing, it was ten times harder to keep hold of her. He placed her inside the doorway and she ran inside, yelling.

"Thank you both so much for your help," I said. "I think we can take it from here." I hurried inside and tried to calm her down.

•••

The next night as the family sat down for dinner, I had to rally Nadya to come eat. She had been playing outside, not ready to come in for dinner. Despite the weekly therapy she was having with Dr. Wilson, not much had changed since we had brought her home. Small things like her eye contact had improved, but still, any transition—big or small—set her off. A tool that works for some traumatized children is setting timers so they can prepare for transitions, but they never worked with Nadya because they only increased her anxiety.

"It's okay, Nadya." I smiled, trying to get her to come towards me. She was storming around the living room, and I tried to put my hand on her shoulder. In response, she twisted away and ran down the hall.

Before I could process what was happening, she ran right to the front door, flung it open, and sprinted outside. She wasn't fast, but it took me a minute to realize she was running away, and I dashed out the door after her. She was already halfway down the block before I caught up with her. I grabbed her shoulders and tried to bring her in close to my body.

"Nadya! Stop running and come to dinner!" I was caught so off guard that I couldn't hide my panic. But she twisted out of my grip and took off again. I shouted, "Nadya, where are you going?"

Karl approached my side in a run, passing me with a swift motion and grabbing her from behind, scooping her tiny twelve-year-old frame off her feet. She weighed barely seventy-five pounds but her violent squirms made it seem double that. She screamed and writhed as he lifted her off her feet and swung her around to bring her back home. She maneuvered away from Karl with boxer-like expertise, twisting and spinning and escaping his grasp. He ran and caught up to her again, holding on tighter this time.

He walked briskly with her back to the house, and each car that passed by gave us curious glances as she bucked and kicked in Karl's arms. It took the rest of the night for her to calm down.

From that point on, every time her emotions started to escalate, she made a beeline for the door. Sometimes I was able to get there before she did and stand in front of it to block her way. She would rush to the back door, and again, if I was lucky, I would put my body between her and the door so she couldn't open it. She hit and kicked me, yelling as she tried to twist the door handle. This was a new level of fear: If I couldn't keep my daughter inside my house, how could I keep her safe?

Despite her new behavior, I continued to let her play in the backyard (although I never let her out of my sight). She quickly learned places she could hide right outside our house where we couldn't see her. If somehow I didn't catch her the moment she ran out the door, she often hid behind a bush or a parked car, making me fear she'd run away again. Ironically, despite the trauma Nadya had experienced and the way her brain had rewired itself to survive, she had no idea what dangers loomed if she found herself lost. We were terrified that she would be kidnapped or assaulted. Finally, realizing that we could no longer guarantee a safe environment for her, we knew we needed to look into other options.

By the end of the summer, we had enrolled in a voluntary social services program through the state known as Reach—which provided us with a care coordinator, family support, and a Mobile Urgent Treatment Team, or MUTT team for short, for which we had an 800 number. They were a team of volunteer psychotherapists who were supposed to respond within thirty minutes to help us resolve any urgent situation we called them for. We tried it a few times, but they either showed up too late or completely floundered when they did arrive. Nadya didn't know who these people were, and she just became more enraged when she realized we were calling for help. We warned the volunteers not to get too close to her when she was raging in the house because they were sure to get hit or kicked, but they never listened. After two or three visits, we decided not to call them again. If Nadya didn't hit or kick them, she hid under the bed until they were gone, full of fear. Did she feel that we were causing all the fear? *Were* we? We questioned ourselves. Were we doing more harm than good? Were we causing her not to trust us?

Dr. Wilson and the people at the Reach program urged us to consider residential care, and while we had fought the idea for years, we could no longer dismiss it. Nadya's rages were so nonstop that on occasion, Dr. Wilson took time out of her schedule to pay a house call, for which we were very grateful.

This evening, fortunately, Nadya hadn't had an explosive rage, so Dr. Wilson, Karl, and I were able to sit at the kitchen table to talk about the current state of our family.

Although the topic of residential care was the elephant in the room, Dr. Wilson knew our resistance, so she led the conversation with alternatives. "Maybe you can get some motion-activated lights or an alarm that will go off if the door is opened," she suggested. "Parents whose children have autism use those."

I didn't think that would help. "Half the time she's outside already and just wanders away. I don't know what to do short of handcuffing myself to her."

"Well," Dr. Wilson began gently, "maybe now is the time to consider other options. Residential care." Gauging my body language, she went on. "It would give you a chance to get your family back together—"

I cut her off. "No, no way." I shook my head. "I'm not putting her back in another institution."

"Maybe you could just think about it," she said. She saw the concern in my eyes and reassured me that we were good parents. "Getting information is not the same as making the decision. I am just asking you to learn about Genesee Lake School . . . then we can talk together about whether or not it could help your family."

She pulled out a trifold brochure for Genesee Lake School and slid it across the table.

"Just read over this and give it some thought. It might be the best option for Nadya's safety and your peace of mind. I promise you that we will work to maintain your relationship with her if you decide that it would be a good fit. In fact, you might find that the planned separation allows you to be more present in your relationship with her."

I could barely lift my head. Tears filled my eyes at the thought that I had failed my daughter so completely that now this was all we were left with—putting her in an institution.

Dr. Wilson reminded me of what she had told me so many times before—that a key to Nadya's healing was that calm, well-regulated caretakers surround her. That she would learn from "co-regulation" and specifically from modeling my physiology. Dr. Wilson made the gentle observation that our family was under such duress that no one was happy or well regulated, and it gave Nadya little hope for improving her own behavior. In residential care, however, trained staff worked within a robust support structure and were able to recharge, without the personal responsibility of twenty-four-hour care. Without this 24/7 responsibility, Dr. Wilson reminded me that I would be more capable of modeling the calm, thoughtful behavior that Nadya needed to make developmental progress and maintain a relational connection with family members.

"I visited Genesee Lake School last month," Dr. Wilson explained. "This is a place where they are going to treat her behavior as a reflection of her overactive stress response. Their program focuses on building therapeutic *relationships* that will help her learn to calm that part of her brain down."

This was exactly how Dr. Wilson had been teaching us to help Nadya heal since the day we met her.

"They are professionals at this," she said, which comforted me. "You shouldn't blame yourself in any way, Lori—you are a phenomenal parent to her. But it's often nearly impossible for a family to do that kind of therapy around the clock."

"It's so hard when you're walking on eggshells all the time," said Karl. He looked at me tentatively, placing a warm hand on my knee as he looked back at Dr. Wilson, exhaustion written all over his face.

"When you have a child in the house whose behavior you can't predict one second to the next . . . she could just go off and come after you. We are fortunate enough that Nadya hasn't done anything to seriously hurt somebody . . . but when she is raging and it's escalating, it's hell. She's a ticking time bomb waiting to go off."

I nodded. What Karl said was true, but I felt a crevasse open up in my heart at the decision with which we were faced. How long could we keep patching the wound, praying it would stop the bleeding but with no evidence there was real healing happening? I felt defeated because the truth was, I just didn't know.

That week, I spent time researching Genesee Lake School online, and to my surprise, it seemed like a regular school: cheery and bright. Thick woods surrounded it on almost every side, and I knew Nadya would like that. I saw they did group outings in controlled settings, similar to field trips, and my heart ached at the thought that my daughter might have a chance to experience some semblance of school the way other kids did. Still, I didn't know how I could actually bring myself to put my daughter in an institution. I knew I had to stop thinking that way. What I needed was not to think of it as an "institution" but rather a safe haven for her, a place that was structured, where she had the possibility to be educated and to meet other girls she could form some kind of relationship with. She would have security around the clock, seven days a week, which eased my mind. We owed it to her to give her the best care possible; we would do it for any of our children.

Most nights, I set her on my lap on our "cozy chair" and we would look at the brochures and pictures I had of GLS. I gauged her reaction. I wasn't sure she completely understood.

"This is a special school where you can learn better than you can right now," I told her.

I showed her the pictures of the woods and asked her what she thought she would find there.

"Bugs!" she answered, wide-eyed.

We hadn't made a decision yet, but once Nadya became familiar with the brochures of this "cool new school," Karl and I decided to take a trip up there to get a better feeling for it.

After a forty-five minute drive, and with Dr. Wilson by our side for support, we arrived. When we first walked up, I was amazed at how, just like the pictures on the website and in the brochure, it felt like a regular school.

The folks in the reception area buzzed us in—which gave me a good sense of security, as I knew Nadya wouldn't be able to run away. There was a front office to the left with no bulletproof glass. The staff greeted us with genuine, warm smiles. Across from the office was another small room where the security officers on duty worked. They didn't wear uniforms that could frighten a child, but instead were dressed in street clothes with friendly name tags. Each one smiled at us as we passed. Immediately, I felt that my daughter would be much safer here than she was at our home, and the school and staff were all pleasant. There was nothing frightening or "institutional" about this place.

The area where the kids lived was segregated—boys on one side of the building and girls in the other wing, with a central gathering place filled with couches and TVs. More than anything, it seemed like a cheerful college dormitory. The staff tour guide explained they had movie nights with popcorn, or spa nights where kids painted their nails on the cushy chairs. On the walls hung colorful pictures and decorations for the upcoming Christmas holiday, and a kids' gym held a treadmill and other kid-friendly exercise equipment. It all seemed so inviting, so different from our experiences at other institutions.

After touring the private rooms, bathrooms, and the safe room (a place where kids could go to scream and blow off steam without getting hurt), we felt as though we had a thorough understanding of the facility.

The entire plan the care coordinator explained to us made a lot of sense; every activity the kids were involved in was structured around relational connection (which helped with emotional regulation), positive behavior support, and therapy (to build personal understanding and social competence). They had a lot of fun activities throughout the day, but also plenty of one-on-one time with a therapist. I especially liked that Nadya would be at the same learning level as the other girls in her class, and that these would be girls at her cognitive level—people she could interact with. The thought that she wouldn't be "different" at Genesee Lake School, the way she had been everywhere else we had tried to send her, warmed me from the inside out. Here she would fit in. She could become a part of a community. She would stand a chance at developing into who we knew she was, apart from the complexities of her disability.

On our drive home, Karl and I spoke very little to each other, both of us processing what we had seen and how it might work for us. Later that night, before dinner, I asked Nadya to come sit on my lap so I could show her more pictures of the library and the sensory room. The sensory room had a swing and a bouncy ball to play with, and kids could go in there and play in their free time.

"They have black squirrels there?" It must have been the tenth time she'd asked as we looked at the grounds in the brochures.

I smiled. "Yes, Nadya, they have black squirrels. You can go for walks in the woods and see them running through the trees."

"I didn't know they have black ones."

"Well, they do, and you can see them there." That seemed to satisfy her. "Would you like to go to school there?"

"No." She shook her head, not defiant but calm and confident. I sighed. She always said no. She didn't want to try new things, as much as I enticed her. I was worried, but I thought about all the ways I could be creative and show her how fun it might be. I knew that once we acknowledged the fears that lay beneath her frequent refusals, she would be more receptive to the possibility.

When one of Logan's friends, on a break from college, came over for dinner a few weeks later, I pulled him aside.

"Eric," I whispered urgently. "Would you please make a point of saying how great college is in front of Nayda? Where you get to live there during the week and come home on weekends? We're trying to help her imagine a school setting where she doesn't live with her family so that the idea of a residential program isn't so scary to her."

Eric nodded. "Sure, Mrs. Hetzel."

"Tell her that it's really cool and great to be in college during the day with your friends and that you only come home on the weekends and holidays." I knew that Eric highlighting this would help Nadya make a concrete connection that her family would remain a part of her, even if she lived in a different place.

Just before dinner, Eric did as I asked. He stood at the counter and picked at the vegetable tray as he told Nadya about how great college was, how he loved being there, and how he came home on the weekends, just like he was now, visiting Logan.

"Hey, you know what, Eric?" I chimed in, feigning surprise. "That sounds a lot like the special school we are thinking about sending Nadya to." I pulled out the brochure and handed it to him, and he looked it over, oohing and aahing. I tentatively watched Nadya during my exchange with Eric; her emotions, as always, were nearly impossible to read.

Karl and I made one more visit to GLS before we made up our minds. After chasing Nadya down the street for months, and nervously watching her every move whenever she was outside, we made the difficult decision to get more help from state social services involved in her care.

Dr. Wilson guided us however she could. "You can go to court and file a non-emergency CHIPS petition. You wouldn't lose custody of your daughter," she explained. "She will still be your child. You'll still maintain your parental rights and be involved in all decisions regarding her needs."

A CHIPS petition, which stood for "Child in Need of Protective Services," is normally filed by a state social worker when a child is in an unsafe home situation and needs to be removed quickly for his or her own safety. We were in an unusual situation because we were the ones filing the petition, essentially asking the state to remove our daughter from our house for her own safety. We couldn't afford to send Nadya to GLS out of pocket, and this was the only way the state would help us cover the cost of this specialized treatment.

Even though we trusted Dr. Wilson, this was the scariest part for me. I was so afraid I would no longer be Nadya's mom, that she would be taken out of our home and be lost in the state system for good—that we might have no way to get her back. It seemed so permanent to me, and the night I realized it was our only option, I cried until my tear ducts effectively dried up.

Would my daughter think we had given up on her? My body rocked against my pillow as I realized that maybe I was secretly afraid that a residential program meant I *had* given up on her. That after all our years of hard work and therapy, we were throwing in the towel.

Over the years, we had heard of residential treatment options for Nadya, but it had always seemed like such a drastic step that we had never seriously considered it. Now, it turned out to be our last hope. Still, as we read about all the programs available from the state—many of them appropriate for children who were delinquent, truant, or on drugs, none of which was the case with Nadya—we had to trust the system. Every night, I faithfully prayed that the judge who saw our case would understand that we were well-intentioned parents of a traumatized child who needed specialized care and resources beyond what we could provide in the home. We believed GLS was the best option for her, and hoped that the judge would place her there.

As awful as that felt, I also worried that the social workers would come into my home and judge me for being a bad parent. I felt like I had failed my child. I couldn't believe that it had come to this, that I would have *Child Protective Services* involved, of my own accord, no less. I had always thought a child was removed due to neglect and abuse, but we called to get relief from and help for our daughter. I was consumed by guilt and fear, but we didn't feel we had another, better, choice.

We initiated the paperwork one tear-filled afternoon at Dr. Wilson's office. The petition addressed our safety and education concerns, and asked for the intensive therapy she needed. We wanted her to develop and grow, and we had not seen that in her yet. In short, we pleaded, we wanted to give Nadya the best we could give her, and we felt GLS was the best place to do it.

Things moved quickly after that. A month later, after

several visits from surprisingly understanding CPS workers, the filing was complete.

One Friday morning not long after the paperwork was submitted, we convened for our court date to decide Nadya's fate. Both Karl and I were terrified, but we tried to remain calm for Nadya, as she was expected to attend as well.

We were told that the judge had looked over all of the paperwork, including the extensive evaluations and recommendation letter Dr. Wilson had provided, and we hoped and prayed that everyone saw we were good parents trying our best, and that we were just out of options.

"Mr. and Mrs. Hetzel," started the judge, looking from left to right in the courtroom. "I understand this is a difficult process for you. I believe your hearts are in the right place and that you are doing the right thing for Nadya."

A flood of relief swept over me as I tried to calm my racing heart.

The judge's papery skin and wise eyes were the caricature of an old judge who had clearly been in the Child Protective Services system a long time. My relief extended even further, as I knew he could tell what was happening in this situation with just one look at us.

"It's clear to me that you are both on the same side when it comes to doing what's right for your little girl. I'm going to support your petition for her admission to GLS," he said.

Oh, thank God, I thought. We were relieved that the court agreed with us on what was good for Nadya; it reinforced the validity of our decision.

My mind raced as the attorneys and the judge worked out the details right before us. To my tear-filled gratitude, they let her come home with us, and we finally had a date: in three weeks, on December 1, 2010, Nadya would enter GLS and start getting the help she needed.

All of our lives were about to change.

CHAPTER 11
NADYA'S NEW HOME AT GENESEE LAKE SCHOOL

Nadya was not happy about going to a new school, and we did the best we could over the next three weeks to prepare her for it. I tried to remain upbeat and excited, although my nerves were on edge.

"You'll have a cool new room, all to yourself," I told her. "It'll be just like college!" She remained unimpressed. Nadya really didn't know what college was, but I reminded her of what Eric had said. We went shopping for new bedding and she picked a comforter with Disney fairies on it.

"Wow, this will look so great in your new room!" I encouraged her, but she never bought into it.

We knew that we wouldn't be able to bring her home at all for the first thirty days. The staff at GLS explained that this would make her overall acclimation much easier. We decided we would start her there on a Wednesday, so that we would be able to come visit her on the weekend just three days later.

The big day finally arrived. Connor wrote her a note that morning before he left for school, saying that he hoped she had a good day and enjoyed her new school.

"I'll see you Saturday," he wrote, and I read it to Nadya.

I hadn't prompted him to write it, but I was so grateful for his act of kindness. Delaney came over to say goodbye before she got on the bus.

"I hope you like your new school," she said, standing awkwardly in front of Nadya. They didn't hug. Nadya silently watched her walk away. I watched Delaney walk to the bus with her head down. I knew she had mixed emotions and didn't quite understand what was happening. I think she was afraid that Nadya was being sent away because she was adopted, and maybe somewhere in the back of her mind, she was afraid she could also be sent to a special school for adopted children. Even though our family dynamic had been so strained, there was still some grieving because everything was again about to change.

We packed up Nadya's suitcase and got her in the car. She was sullen and withdrawn on the way to the school. Even stopping for a milkshake didn't improve her mood. She sat in the back, nervously picking at her nails.

A team of her caretakers met us in the lobby to get us checked in. First we had to go over some logistics, like reviewing her medications with a nurse. Nadya sat by my side, crying softly, confused by what was happening.

"It's okay, Nadya, honey," I kept trying to reassure her. "This is a special school where you are really going to learn." I patted her on the leg and stroked her hair.

"Remember we talked all about the black squirrels and bugs and birds here?" I reminded her. "Delaney doesn't have black squirrels at her school. You are one lucky girl."

She barely seemed to register what I was saying.

"Honey, Mommy and Daddy just want what's best for you," I added, but nothing could console her. My heart ached for her, pounding so hard that I could feel it in my ears. I was holding back tears that were beginning to sting my eyes. I couldn't let her see me cry. This was supposed to be something wonderful for her.

"Look at all this beautiful art on the walls!" I gestured to the colorful paintings that lined the hallway, which had been created by the children of the school. "You're going to get to do so many fun things here, and learn a lot, too." No matter how much I tried to soothe her, I had no luck. The nurse smiled at me knowingly and gave me a reassuring nod.

We sat down with her care coordinator, Beth, who would be our main point of contact for all of Nadya's treatment during her time at GLS. Together, we carefully reviewed our expectations for her care. I explained that foremost among my hopes was an end to the rages. They had driven me to the point of insanity over the past three and a half years, and I just wanted them to stop. I explained to Beth that we lived in constant fear—that I was afraid to wake up. I heard myself saying I was afraid of being hit and bit all the time, and that GLS was our only hope.

"Of course, working on helping Nadya regulate her emotions is a big goal for all of us here," Beth started. "But as you know more than anyone, Mrs. Hetzel, it will first take time for Nadya to build trusting relationships with her new caretakers."

"I know. I know how hard it is for her to trust anybody new," I said.

"Exactly. And many of our children here have that issue. Because of that, many of them will get worse before they get better," she continued. "I just want you to be prepared for that. It will very likely take months to establish trust, before we can even begin to think about making any progress on the cognitive and emotional fronts."

I knew what she was saying was true—it would take time for Nadya to get used to anybody. I knew that if she felt abandoned, she would regress, and I redoubled my determination to not let her feel that way.

"We want to make sure Nadya won't feel that we just left her here," I said. "We are here to participate one hundred percent in her care. Just tell me what I need to do."

"Well, first of all, you can call her whenever you like. Here is the number to reach me, and here is the direct number to her pod, or dormitory. One of the staff in Nadya's wing will always answer this number, and you can talk to your daughter in the mornings or evenings when she's not in class."

I nodded, grateful that it would be so easy to get a hold of her.

Beth went on to explain how every single aspect of a child's care at GLS was administered in a closed system where all caretakers knew and embraced sensitive, trauma-informed care.

"All of our staff have been specifically trained in working with traumatized children," she explained. "It's not just her teachers or therapists, but the people who help her shower and get dressed, too. The people who serve her lunch—all of them understand the special needs of children that come to us."

It was such a relief—this was exactly what I needed to hear.

"We want you to know that we do all of this with the goal of discharge one day in the not-too-distant future;

we want to make sure that everyone in the family knows and understands what discharge will look like—what conditions have to be met to get there. That is always our goal from day one. We want to work with your family and make sure you have the support and therapy you need as well. We want to make sure your family has a plan for the future."

"Thank you," I said. "We appreciate that. We just want her to get better so she can come home, too."

Next we spoke with the psychologist who would be having weekly sessions with Nadya, and he explained to me in more concrete details the specific goals they would be working on, although he, too, warned me that it would likely be many months before we saw real progress.

"I've reviewed all of the paperwork you and Karl have filled out, and I just wanted to let you know that we are on the same page as far as expectations," he began. "I know that for Nadya, like for most of our children here, transitions are a big problem area, so we really focus on making sure they are in a completely structured and routine environment that is the same every day. When they know exactly what to expect, they do much better." He went on to explain that Nadya would be assigned to a girls' pod that did everything together. They would transition from task to task in a single-file line. If one girl needed to go to the bathroom, everybody would stop and wait for her.

"We'll be setting weekly goals for her for things like how long it takes her to get dressed and shower in the morning, how many positive peer interactions she had, did she initiate conversations, did she exhibit any aggression—those are the things we'll be watching out for and working with her on to develop skills to improve."

Wow. These people really have it together; they really know what they're doing. The thought made me so happy—that she would be completely enveloped in this level of care. I could already see that maybe, just maybe, Nadya would thrive here. Nadya was sitting on my lap, looking at the strangers seated with us at the long wooden table. I held her hand, squeezing her little fingers lightly to reassure her. This was the kind of precise, structured care that was nearly impossible to give in the confines of our home, with its many people and variables. As I had begun to learn, it is often the unexpected that makes these children completely unwind.

The staff didn't use terms like "RAD" as much as they referred to the traumatic early childhood Nadya and children like her experienced. I appreciated their sensitivity to the complexity of her case. I felt a huge weight being lifted off my shoulders as, paradoxically, it all started to sink in. I looked at Karl. His shoulders, too, seemed to relax as he listened intently to what was being discussed.

Nadya's therapy here would be so much more than just an hour-long session once a week. Every interaction and relationship was structured so that she could learn the skills she needed to function in the world: getting along with others, learning how to interact with people, working as a group—all things she desperately needed.

"Our treatment is very much informed by Bruce Perry's work on what happens to children when they are born into not just a neglectful situation but something worse—pathogenic care," Nadya's psychologist continued. "When a child's basic needs aren't met, it compromises brain development."

I was familiar with these ideas already, but I was eager to hear how GLS approached them.

"These children are traumatized from a young age, which is why we refer to their experience as a *complex developmental trauma* situation—it's almost like they have PTSD, but it's not the acute kind you would think of in a war veteran. What children like Nadya have is a brain that has been compromised because of the trauma they experienced. Their brains have physically not developed normally. This is why her overall adaptive skill development is inhibited."

Nadya's body began to stiffen on my lap. I am certain she was wondering why everyone was talking about her. They smiled at her to ease her fear, but she met them with mean eyes. This was all technical language and she didn't know what to do with herself. She was getting squirmy and I kept hoping it wouldn't take much longer. It was hard enough on all of us, but we needed to discuss the importance of her treatment. I searched my purse for some gum and offered her my last piece, which she was happy to accept.

"What separates RAD children from other types of PTSD sufferers is that their trauma was intentional, prolonged, and relational. It is caused by caregivers who intentionally and continuously neglect a child's basic needs—this is a *created* disorder, and our staff here understand that. These kids are not born this way. Almost universally, RAD children have brains that have rewired themselves almost exclusively for fight, flight, or freeze."

Karl sighed, fidgeting with the brochure he held. "Believe me, we have spent three and a half years learning that the hard way," he said, nodding. "It is so deeply rooted in her—and nothing we've tried has really helped." He cleared his throat and took a moment to collect his composure.

"We love our little Dinks," he said softly, and went on to explain that this was our nickname for her. She was so dinky when we first met her, and she still is. There was a momentary lapse of quiet. "I'm sorry, go on," he said.

"That's really a neat nickname, Nadya," said Beth.

Nadya refused to make eye contact with her.

"Well, here, the core of our trauma-sensitive practices for these kids revolves around recognizing that their trauma reaction is an adaptation," the psychologist chimed in. "It is a symptom of what they have gone through. We need to build skills now—we need to find out what skill challenges they lack, which are usually emotion regulation and problem solving, and work with them to figure out how to solve the problems they face throughout their day," he said, and I appreciated his plain language. "Basically, what we need to do with these children is to change their version of self, others, and the world. I think it is that simple, and that hard—because those versions they have in their heads right now are not very good."

I nodded, though I still couldn't quite wrap my brain around how they would be able to change those things when we had been trying for years with little success.

"The damage done to these kids is in how they relate, and so the question we ask ourselves is how do you fix that through relationships?" he explained. "The answer is through therapeutic relationships—which are relationships where everyone interacting with the child recognizes the trauma. That's the relational element of what we do. It also has to be repetitive and rhythmic—which is why we use a lot of dance and music. We find they're a good way to bring children out of their shell and help reorganize the brain."

"That makes sense," I said. "Nadya has always responded well to music—she loves her iPod." I also liked the idea that she would be surrounded by other girls working on the same things—maybe it would motivate her.

"You know, we did try some of this at home," I ventured. "We played volleyball with a balloon. She enjoyed it, but soon got tired of that game and refused to do it again. Then I tried to play catch with her, but her motor skills are poor, and she soon gave up on that too. I sat on the floor with a real potato to play 'hot potato,'—you know, rolling the potato back and forth as fast as you can. She giggled but again gave up shortly thereafter." I sighed.

"That's very impressive," said the psychologist.

"Well, I'm hoping it will be more fun and helpful to her here," I said, smiling.

Nadya rose from my lap as if she were ready for us to go home. She just stood there looking at me. I don't think she realized that this was it, that this would be her home now. She moved towards the frost-covered window and looked out at the frozen ground.

"Our main goal is to help her learn to regulate—and we try to work with the kids to develop regulation strategies that will work for them. We use an occupational therapist and employ a lot of sensory strategies like deep pressure, skin brushing, weighted vests—those kinds of things. Things that work well with autism also work well for kids like Nadya. She, like many of the other kids here, is always hypersensitive, so for instance, even when we have a fire drill, our trauma-informed approach is to give all the kids advance notice and maybe give headphones to the kids who need them. We try to take that approach in everything we do with them."

Karl scooted his chair closer to me and took my hand. He looked at me and smiled. "That all sounds so smart, so well thought-out," he said.

"We do our best," the psychologist said with a small smile. "It's never an easy road."

Karl asked him how the pods were arranged in regards to what kind of girls Nadya would be living with.

"Her pod will be made up of girls who match her age, disability, demeanor, and social skills—those kinds of things. But she will attend class with people who are cognitively at her level, in mixed grades, so that we are catering to her level of learning. However, we probably won't start her in school right away. There is often too much stimulation for kids when they first come here, so we just try to get them comfortable with the environment and the staff. Usually we wait a few weeks before we put them in the actual classroom."

I knew that long before you can begin to teach a child skills to cope with their emotions, you have to spend time every day doing things like playing checkers with them, and I knew that's what the GLS staff would have to do first, too.

We also knew Nadya needed structure and boundaries—I hoped with every fiber of my being that she would give this place a chance, while I simultaneously felt bad knowing she had no say in the decision our family had made. All of the structure and routine here was the antidote to the chaotic, unpredictable situations she had faced at a young age, which had made her brain develop the way it had. This was our chance to put our family back together, and we were committed, no matter how long it could take.

Nadya moved slowly back onto my lap.

"Did you see any black squirrels outside, Nadya?" I asked.

She refused to answer. She gave me a worried look and tugged at my coat. "I wanna go home, Mom."

"I know, sweetie. We are here learning all about your school though. Why don't you sit by the window? Take this chair, honey."

"No," was her only reply.

The staff went on to explain that Nadya would be entitled to a small spending stipend from the state, which she could use on outings. She would earn the right to go with staff members to places like Target or Walmart when she met her goals for the week. This was also part of teaching her skills—teaching her how to make positive decisions about what she would like to buy. Nadya spoke for the first time.

"I get money?" she asked curiously.

"Yes," Beth said. "You can go shopping and get whatever you want.

Nadya looked stumped.

"Isn't that cool, Nadya?" I said to her. "You'll be able to go to the store and spend your *own* money. Don't you think that'll be so neat?" I was so grateful they would be doing real-world activities with the children. I had to reinforce to Nadya that at Delaney's school, she didn't get money or go shopping.

"That is cool," she replied. "Delaney doesn't get money?"

"Nope," I said. "None."

Nadya smiled for the first time.

I handed Nadya my phone so she could play some games while we continued our meeting. This seemed to help pass the time for her. Her psychologist went on to explain that she needed skills to cope with life, not discipline or punishment.

"That's what we're here to teach her. We're going to work together with Nadya—because it's a collaborative process—to find tools and systems that work for her. We'll help her identify and develop potential solutions, but in the end, she is the one who gets to make the decision. The more involved she becomes in finding solutions to her own emotional upheavals, the better it will work for her."

"We've never really been able to discipline her at home," I said. "You know, like the usual grounding? She doesn't understand that process. It would only escalate the situation. Of course, this was one of the big areas Delaney and Connor did not understand," I said, lowering my voice to a whisper so Nadya wouldn't hear. "They got grounded. They had things taken away. She never did. It caused a lot of problems at home because here she was the one who was physically attacking and she never saw any consequences." I glanced at Nadya, who was deeply focused on her game.

"They hated her for it," I added.

The group nodded thoughtfully. "I'm sure it was very hard for everyone, Mrs. Hetzel," the psychologist said, and I truly felt that these people understood.

I went on to say that it would take Nadya longer not only to trust the staff, but also to communicate.

"We understand, Mrs. Hetzel," Beth said. "It will take time, and we do have the time to dedicate to Nadya."

Dedicate. I repeated the word in my head. *That has a nice ring to it.*

This was a marvelous introduction to the care our daughter would now be receiving. I felt lighter with each passing moment.

. . .

The next step was to get Nadya moved in. We took her down to the laundry room, where they had prepared special name tags that would go on all of her clothes and belongings, which wouldn't come off in the wash. We took her to the lunchroom so she could meet the staff there and see where she would eat every day.

"Wow, what a neat lunch room, Nadya," I began. "What do you think? Delaney's lunchroom isn't this nice." I had to say these things to make it seem that Delaney was the one missing out—it was the one thing that seemed to work with Nadya.

She just shrugged her shoulders.

Next, we headed up to her pod. I kept my eye on Nadya to see her reaction. She seemed curious but did not ask any questions. Karl and I took turns saying how neat this school was and how she would really be learning here.

On the wall, a big board was laid out with every day's exact schedule, complete with picture cues. We observed that several nights they had group activities planned, like movies and popcorn and spa nights.

"Wow, Nadya, I never got to do this when I went to school."

Karl was impressed, too. He knew this would be the place where our little girl would finally get the help she so deserved. He turned to me and said, "Feel better now?"

"Yes, this is great, honey. I feel so much better. We made the right decision."

Nadya just stood there in her purple winter coat, picking at her nails with her head down.

We continued down the hall to her bedroom. A bright name tag on the door said "Welcome, Nadya Hetzel!"

"Look Nadya," Karl said. "This is pretty cool, huh? They're happy to have you at your new school."

"Wow, Nadya, how special is that?" I commented.

We had Nadya choose where she would like to hang the posters of horses and unicorns that she had brought with her. Karl took off the bedding and replaced it with the Disney fairies comforter.

"Look, Nadya, see how pretty your room is?" I said.

She remained quiet.

I went over to the window and beamed at her. "Look at that," I said, pointing. "Do you see what is right outside there?"

Nadya looked out the window, somewhat interested. "Woods," she said finally.

"That's right, woods!" I said. "Think about how you can see the woods anytime you want, even from your window. Oh, look, there's a black squirrel!" I said excitedly.

"Really?" she asked.

I prayed. *Please God, help her find the help she needs . . . please.*

"I see it!" she exclaimed. "It's black. Oh, it is so cute! So cute, Mama!"

"Sweetie, we have to leave now, but we'll see you in

three days," I said to her. "You can mark the days on the calendar I gave you." I had highlighted Saturday so she would know which day we were coming to visit her. "Just three days, and we'll see you."

Nadya looked at the calendar, sad and forlorn, and back at me with tears in her eyes. She wrapped her arms around me and started crying softly. "Don't go," she whispered. "Please. I'm scared, Mama. Why do I have to stay here?"

"Shh, it's going to be okay," I told her, hugging her back and kissing the top of her head. I tried to make my voice sound cheerful and strong as I repeated how much fun she would have here, but I was breaking down inside, too. The staff gal standing next to us looked on with a tender smile.

"Hey, Nadya, I want to show you something," she chimed in, for which I was grateful. "Do you like to play Wii?"

Nadya looked at her tentatively, wiping her tears away. *Yes, she loves to play Wii,* I thought. Nadya gave a small nod.

"Do you want to come play with me on the TV in the big common room?"

"Okay," said Nadya, and just like that, she took the woman's hand and headed down the hallway. She didn't even look back.

"Bye, Nadya," I yelled after her, but she kept going.

"That wasn't that hard," Karl said, visibly relieved and surprised.

We quietly made our exit and drove home with a mixture of emotions that told us we were doing everything right—despite the guilty feeling that lingered.

CHAPTER 12
A NEW BEGINNING

Almost as soon as I got home, I wanted to call her. The care coordinator had told us how important it was for children at GLS to feel that their parents are still involved in their care, for them to still understand that they are part of a family, that they haven't been abandoned. Some children feel like they are re-experiencing the trauma from their early childhood, and the staff at GLS had warned us to try to prevent that with frequent contact and visits. That first night's call was just a few minutes, but I got in what I wanted to say.

"You are in a really good place now, honey," I told her when the staff member handed her the phone. "You are going to get a lot of help and meet new friends, and soon you'll be able to come home on the weekends. And you can count on us being there Saturday—we're already excited to come visit you."

"I want to come home." Her voice was timid and shaky.

"Soon, honey, soon."

...

I was eager to visit her that first Saturday, and we arrived early in the morning. We were shown into a small private room off the main lobby that had two couches and some chairs, with a window looking out over the woods. I was so nervous to see her. *Will she hate us for leaving her there? Will she ever forgive us?* My stomach was tied in knots.

Someone from Nadya's pod brought her down to us, showed her in, and then left us in private.

"Hi, honey, how are you?" I rushed in, eager to put my arms around her but first waiting to judge how she was doing. She wouldn't look at us and silently sat down on the couch opposite where we sat.

"Tell us all about your new school, Nadya," I said, my voice cheerful. "How do you like it?"

She continued to stare out the window. "Am I going home now?" she asked flatly. My heart sank.

"Honey," I began softly, "not yet. You are going to be at this school for a while. This is the best place for you to be. You're really going to get help with feeling better here."

"I want to go home. I don't like it here. I want Zoe. I want my dog," she said all at once.

"I know, honey, we all miss you, but you will see Zoe soon, I promise."

She looked at me with sullen eyes and a flat expression.

"Dad bought you a strawberry shake, Nadya," I said, changing the subject.

She reached over and grabbed it out of his hand. I reminded her to say thank you, but she returned to staring out the window, her voice and face almost entirely disengaged from our presence. *Almost*, which was the key to our hopefulness.

For the rest of our forty-five minutes together, she

barely said a word. She seemed resigned and offered up few details about how her first days had gone.

"I'll call you as soon as I get home," I told her, as I was already in the habit of calling her several times a day just to say hello. We reassured her that we loved her and that starting next month, she could come home for visits on the weekends. I knew from the phone call I had had with a staff member the day before that she had been mostly quiet the last few days and that there had been no major episodes.

My sad little girl sat across from me, and I knew the one thing she wanted right now—to come home—I couldn't give her. She barely made eye contact, was cold and distant, and we were consumed with fear that she was starting to regress . . . and that we had made a serious mistake in sending her here.

...

Back at home, we experienced our first real vacation from the trauma that we had experienced for the last three and a half years. Right away, ninety-nine percent of the stress that permeated our household evaporated. Nadya was gone, and she wouldn't be home for a long time. For the first time in years, I could walk around my house without the fear of setting off an explosion. Our other children had been through hell with Nadya's rages, and now that there was peace and quiet at home, it was time to mend some of the damage that had been done.

Logan, our oldest, was twenty years old and living on his own, but he started coming home more on the weekends and to have dinner with the family. I felt like I had more time now to get to know him as an adult. I also got to work on reconnecting with Connor and Delaney. One morning at breakfast, Delaney asked me if I missed Nadya.

"Of course I do, sweetie," I replied. "Why do you ask? You know we had to place her there so she can get the help she needs, right?" I explained that she would be learning how to control her feelings so that she wasn't angry all the time.

Delaney nodded thoughtfully but was quiet.

"I know it has been really hard for you all this time," I said, placing my hand on her arm. "You have given up so much for your sister. Sharing toys, giving up your video time so she could play longer. I know how scared you were for me, too," I added, kissing her forehead. "We didn't want you to have to go through any of this, and I am sorry you had to. I am so sorry, Delaney," I repeated as I felt myself choking up.

Delaney stared into her bowl of oatmeal, and then she began to cry. "I hope she gets better, Mommy. She must be so sad and scared to be away from us."

I reached over and pulled her into my lap. "I love you, baby," I said, rocking my youngest child in my lap. "I love you."

...

For the first time in years, Delaney sang again as she walked around the house. She had friends over for sleepovers, which hadn't happened since before we adopted Nadya close to four years earlier. Meanwhile, Connor could play video games in the living room without headphones on. I didn't wake up in the morning terrified that I would hear Nadya's angry pounding footsteps in the bedroom above my head, a sure sign that she was filling with anger and that a rage was coming my way. I no longer had to take an anti-anxiety pill just to have the strength to get out of bed. The mornings were peaceful. It was so good I almost wanted to pinch myself.

I also had a chance to catch up on one of my favorite pastimes—reading for pleasure. I immersed myself in the historical novels that I had always loved, no longer compelled to spend any free moment reading about adoption or children and behavior. I also spent hours just browsing through thick volumes of art history in bookstores, enjoying a cup of coffee and beautiful pictures, just because I could. It was a time of profound healing from all the desperation and noise that had defined our household for years. Laughter returned to our home, and family dinners were pleasant. Everyone talked about their day, took turns, ate their food—the simple things that make life so wonderful.

"This is what a family is supposed to feel like," I said to Karl one night as we were getting into bed.

"I know," he said with a deep breath.

"It's weird not having her here, though, isn't it?" he added. "Do you feel like I do?"

"Of course I do," I said. "It's strange, all these feelings—the good and the bad, it's just . . . it's hard." I struggled to articulate what I was feeling. "No more police in the driveway, no more embarrassing scenes in front of the neighbors . . ." My voice trailed off as I let all the goodness soak in, but we were both aware of the nagging mixed feelings about putting her in the school.

Those first few weeks carried with them a big sense of *Wow, this is a relief!* Guilt swiftly followed. *Am I a bad mother because of the relief I feel that Nadya is gone?* I wondered often. It was hard, and it wasn't clear that we had made the right decision. The emotions were so strong on both sides.

One thing, though, was clear—we were doing the right thing for our other kids. That Christmas was the first time in three years that we had a normal holiday at home. Each year, opening presents was incredibly stressful because Nadya was obsessed with making sure that Delaney didn't have more presents than she had. We had to get the girls the exact same things—there couldn't be a slight deviation or Nadya would throw a fit. No matter how hard we tried, Christmas morning had always turned out to be a nightmare.

But that year, we were relaxed and happy and everything was wonderful. I could hardly remember the last time I had seen Delaney so happy—her eyes all lit up at the attention she was receiving. All the unique and special gifts we showered on her, without her having to worry that Nadya would ruin the day for us, helped make it one of the best holiday seasons I could remember.

...

The first time Nadya came home, after thirty days at GLS, we were all nervous. There was a sense of foreboding—would she willingly get in the car on Sunday to go back to school? Would she fight us? We prayed for the best, and Nadya was so happy to be home, we hoped she would be easy to handle.

Just having her walk in the front door brought the anxiety level back up to where it had been before she left. Everyone was on the lookout for land mines the minute she set foot in the house.

Surprisingly, she was on her best behavior.

"Zoe!" she yelled when she walked in. "Hi, Zoe!" she greeted our dog, who jumped up and down, tail wagging.

"See, Nadya, I told you that you would see Zoe again," I smiled. "She missed you, too."

That evening, we watched a movie as a family, and she actually sat on Karl's lap, which she had never done before. We had made it clear from the start that she would be returning to GLS on Sunday night, and we showed her the calendar and marked the days she would be home, highlighting the day she would be returning to school. She didn't seem thrilled about it, but she didn't say anything to resist it, either.

On Sunday, Karl and I drove together to drop Nadya off, and to our surprise, she got out of the car when we parked.

I yelled to Nadya, "First one to the doorbell wins!" Off she ran to the front door.

"I won! I won, Mama!"

"Yes, you did, Nads, good job!" I complimented her. "Now we need to talk into the speaker for them to let us back in."

She pushed the intercom button.

"Hello," a voice from inside answered. It was Ted, who worked in security and whom Nadya seemed to think was funny. She started giggling.

"It's the Hetzels. We're dropping off Nadya," I said.

"Just a minute, be right there." Ted arrived at the door and let us in. "How are you folks today? Packers are winning!" he said.

"Yay!" I said, looking at Karl and knowing he wished he was at home watching the game.

"Nadya, did you have a nice home visit?" asked Ted. It took her a while, but she finally nodded.

"That's great," he replied. "I'll make a call up to the unit, and someone will be down to get her," he added.

"Thanks, Ted." I smiled.

Nadya went into the lobby and sat down on a brown leather chair. Karl put her small suitcase down and paced back and forth in the hallway. I went to sit on the arm of the chair to snuggle closer to her. She sat there without saying a word.

"I wonder what you'll do today," I said to Nadya. "Do you girls do something on Sunday afternoons?"

She shrugged her shoulders. "I don't know."

"Maybe we will find out when Beth comes to get you," I said. "We are very proud of you, Nadya. You're a brave girl. I need you to know that," I said, looking in her eyes.

Beth came down with a smile on her face. "Nadya, I missed you! Did you have a good home visit? What did you do?"

Nadya didn't reply right away, but finally she said, "It was good. We had movie night. It was really nice."

Beth beamed at her.

"What do you guys do here on Sunday afternoons?" I asked Beth.

"Well, some of the girls are doing arts and crafts, playing games, or just spending quiet time."

Beth turned to Nadya and said, "Nadya, want to play Wii with me?"

Nadya's eyes lit up and she grinned with excitement. She darted up and took off with a smiling Beth down the hall.

"I'll call you before bed!" I yelled after her, and she

waved at me. I still could not believe how well this transition was going.

"Karl, is that our Nadya?" I asked.

"I believe it is," he said, grinning at me.

"Wow, look at her go! That's amazing." A feeling of warmth and gratitude filled my heart.

Still, it was another two months before we truly believed that we had made the right decision for Nadya. There weren't any big changes in her behavior, but I could feel in my heart that this environment, with its stability and sensitivity built in, was the best place for her. She wasn't regressing, which was a good sign. I knew she needed to get well in order for us to have any chance to incorporate her into our lives—for us to have any chance to function as a family.

Nadya got into the routine of coming home on weekends. Karl would pick her up Fridays after work. Slowly, after several months, we noticed that while she still constantly resisted us, she was no longer raging as much as she used to. It was a signpost that we were heading in the right direction. I think in part she thought that she needed to behave well in order to keep coming home, and that helped her regulate her emotions while away from GLS.

I got into a routine of calling the pod every evening when I came home from work. I got to know the staff working the floor and they would give me daily updates—whether she'd had a good day that day, or had trouble in the shower, or helped another girl put together a puzzle. I always felt informed on how she was doing, and then I talked to Nadya each day as well.

For the most part, Nadya continued to do well on her

weekend visits home. If she had issues, I would call the school to speak with Beth or one of the other staff members to let them know of the problem and how we were dealing with it so that when we arrived back, the staff would be prepared to talk to Nadya about it. Nadya did not always want to problem solve right away but was rewarded with Wii when she did. There were a few occasions when Nadya's behavior at home escalated and we brought her back to the school a day early. GLS was always willing to accommodate, for which I was grateful. We felt like we had a team of true allies on our side. All everyone wanted was to see Nadya get better, and she was well on her way.

CHAPTER 13
PROGRESS

Within a year, the unmistakable signs of Nadya's progress were all around us. It was clear the training she was receiving in self-regulating her behavior was having an impact—she could now often stop herself before she raged. Although her behavior was still often rigid and defiant, the amount of time she spent flat-out screaming dramatically decreased.

One of the most important tools Nadya learned at GLS was the emotional scale. Traumatized children often have trouble understanding and quantifying emotions—their own and others'. At GLS, they developed an image-based system, with pictures that ranged from happy (a level "1") to red-faced raging (a level "5"). When Nadya started to feel bad or uncomfortable, she was taught to look at the scale and try to match a picture with the way she was feeling. Studying this scale brought her an awareness that she was starting to feel worse and gave her a way to communicate that with others. As Dr. Wilson had pointed out to us so many times before, the emotional turmoil is hardest on the child who has been traumatized for most of her life. We knew that Nadya hated the rages, but they were all she knew. The emotional scale was a way for her to build awareness around her own state of mind—something that she had never properly developed before.

The corollary to this exercise was to help Nadya develop measures she could draw on when she realized her emotions were going up the scale. Her therapist worked with her to draw pictures of things that she decided helped her at every stage, and they worked to incorporate tools that included all five senses. Some self-calming tools included looking at specific pictures of some of her favorite things, such as musician Keith Urban, horses, or cars, which made her feel better. They would also incorporate things she liked to smell that made her feel calm, or sounds that helped her regulate, and so on. This was one of the core aspects of the GLS focus on "building skills" for developmentally traumatized children, instead of engaging in behavioral-based care, which focuses more on reward and punishment.

A great example of this was that the staff at GLS worked with Nadya to specifically define things that would make her feel better when she was at a level 3. They wouldn't just tell her what to do—they would ask her to come up with her own solutions. Two of the things that worked well for Nadya were putting on her headphones to listen to Keith Urban music, and going into the quiet room by herself. The staff gushed to me how well she self-regulated on days when she felt her emotions rising, and my heart beamed with pride.

What's more is that sometimes when I talked to Nadya in the evening, she would report certain episodes to me.

"How was your day, honey?" I would begin. "What did you do today?"

"Well, today Ellie started throwing crayons at the teacher," she told me once. "She really shouldn't do that. She should go to the quiet room."

With this awareness also came a newfound ability to *not* react to other people's negative behavior. There were other girls in her pod whom I knew lashed out or screamed, and Nadya was able to understand that this behavior wasn't a threat to her, and she would just observe quietly. One time a girl even pulled her hair, and the staff reported that besides saying "Ow!" Nadya hadn't had any adverse reaction to the girl—she just understood the girl was not doing the right thing. I never failed to tell her how proud I was of her when her caretakers told me she had behaved really well that day. She knew that I always knew how she was doing.

Those signs of her increasing awareness—and her ability to distinguish right behavior from wrong behavior—were such rays of hope in my heart. Previously, she had rarely showed remorse or even understanding when she did something "wrong," and we could see that that was starting to change.

As Dr. Wilson had explained to us from the beginning, the main way Nadya was going to heal and rewire her brain was to develop therapeutic relationships that were consistent and sensitive to her trauma, and this was what GLS staff were focused on doing. They used a variety of therapies, and there were some rewards involved, including things like off-campus trips, but the main focus was on building steady, therapeutic relationships with everyone she interacted with. The goal was that everyone at GLS would interact with children in a way that did not make them feel threatened—and so did not trigger them.

Nadya developed a special relationship with her classroom teacher, Ms. Jade, in particular. For the first time, I could sense that Nadya was making real progress in her education. Ms. Jade reported that Nadya was a kind, conscientious, and helpful student, and Karl and I felt such hope for her future. Nadya frequently drew pictures for other students and was often Ms. Jade's "special helper," helping Ms. Jade put away class materials at the end of the day. In our quarterly meetings, Ms. Jade reported that Nadya had become good at asking to go for walks with her when she was feeling bad—she knew walking the hallways with Ms. Jade would make her feel better.

During this time, Nadya was thirteen years old, and while cognitively delayed, physically she was starting to go through puberty, with all the attendant moodiness and crankiness that went with it. Sometimes when it was tough for her to get out of bed in the morning, it was hard to distinguish whether it was defiant behavior or just the age-appropriate response of a teenager who doesn't want to go to school. Also, she got her period during a weekend visit home, and it was quite traumatic for her. She came into my bedroom one Saturday morning and told me the news. I cringed—I had been dreading this day.

I hopped out of bed and went into the bathroom with her. She was trembling.

"Remember the class you took in school about your period?" I reminded her. "Every girl gets one. Mama had one, Delaney does, too. You don't have to be afraid."

"My stomach hurts, and I am dizzy," she said, looking at me shakily.

"I know, Nadya. I know you're scared." She did not understand why this was happening. "You are *not* hurt," I reassured her. "Once a month this will happen, and it's perfectly normal."

She started to cry. "I don't like it, Mama—I don't want it."

"I know, honey. It's just a part of growing up," I said as I hugged her. "Man, oh man, I wish I were a man; then we wouldn't get a period," I joked with her.

She laughed briefly but then looked at me, confused. "They don't?" she asked. It was too much for her to comprehend. A "normal" teen girl understands, but Nadya doesn't. Mentally, she was a second-grader with a period.

The next thing was to teach her how to use a pad. She kept putting it on and taking it off over and over again because it wasn't "perfect." She would get off the toilet and pull her pants up, then immediately lower them, sit back down on the toilet and take the pad off. I tried to explain that it would feel a little uncomfortable at first, but that every girl feels just like she did.

"Nadya, you cannot keep taking off the pads and wasting them," I finally said, exasperated. I looked at the floor, where all of the wrappers and pads were strewn, and cringed.

"We won't have any left now," I told her. "Here is one more. Put it on and get your pants up. I will help you if you need me to."

She put it on and pulled up her pants and walked out of the bathroom with her knees together.

"Why are you walking like that, Nadya? You can walk normally, you know," I said.

"No, I can't," she replied. She would continue to shuffle around with her knees glued together whenever she got her period from then on. I called Delaney into the family room so she could tell Nadya how she hated her period too, and it was interesting to see them interacting on this topic, almost like normal sisters would. But Nadya still seemed to go to the bathroom every ten minutes to check her pad and change it. I tried my best to tell her it would be okay and that I would let her know the next time she should recheck it, but she was too anxious to listen to me. This was not going to be an easy thing for either of us to manage.

• • •

At GLS, Ms. Jade was always a source of calm for Nadya, and Nadya knew that when she was having tummy aches in class, Ms. Jade would pull out a yoga mat for her to lie on so she could still participate. Eventually, she became confident in asking for comfort measures like that, but her monthly period was still traumatic for her. It was especially important for her to shower every day during this time, and Nadya *hated* taking showers. At home, I would have to stand just outside the tub and even wash her hair for her. But at GLS, the staff was supportive but firm, and required her to shower at least every other day on her own. It was so hard for her, often resulting in enormous meltdowns, that within six months we realized it would be best to put Nadya on medication that would stop her period altogether—she just wasn't ready to deal with it.

She displayed other age-appropriate behavior, like teasing children, or boys, and Ms. Jade also worked with her to help her understand when something she said could be perceived differently by another student.

"I explained to Nadya that when she doesn't respond to someone when they talk to her, they could think it means she doesn't like them," Ms. Jade told us during one of our quarterly update meetings.

"She seemed confused by that, explaining it's not that she doesn't like them. I told her that I knew that was true, but not everyone did. I told her when she doesn't feel like talking because of a tummy ache or something like that, she could just say 'I'm tired' or 'I'm cranky right now,' and everyone would understand. She's gotten so much better at reporting on her own state and feelings—I'm really proud of her," beamed Ms. Jade.

Ms. Jade also said Nayda had a noticeable sense of humor. I knew that she could be very funny at times, and seemed to enjoy giving us a chuckle at home on occasion. I loved it when she made me laugh and I told her she was so funny and silly.

"I am?" she would reply, uncertain. But it was clear she was, and she also liked making other children laugh, whether by making faces or telling them a knock-knock joke. Ms. Jade was also impressed that Nadya was developing real social skills with other kids in her class. This was yet another step forward, and we felt happy that she was forming some relationships, knowing this was extremely difficult for her.

Ms. Jade sent home a heartwarming report one weekend on an assignment they had to do in class. Everyone had to go around the room and say one thing they would do for every person in the country if they were president of the United States. Some kids said they would make sure everyone had a house, or a car, and Ms. Jade wrote down Nadya's thoughtful response for us to read:

"I would make sure everybody has a family."

I completely choked up, letting it sink in that my little girl knew I hadn't abandoned her, that we were still her family.

...

"Dad," Nadya said to him one weekend when she was home. "Can I read you my book?"

Karl looked at her, surprised and warmed. "Well, of course you can, honey," he said, bending down in front of her. "I would love that."

The two of them went over to the couch, and she crawled into his lap. I could tell Karl still had a sense of awkwardness at this new experience, but was overjoyed she felt safe enough to be with him in this way. I stood in the family room with a smile on my face as I watched the two of them—Daddy and his daughter.

Nadya opened her simple, second-grade-level book and started reading. It may have only been the equivalent of "See Jane Run," but as he caught my eye out of his peripheral vision, I could tell he was as positively shocked as I was.

A few weekends later, another shock came.

"Mom," Nadya said to me one Saturday afternoon when she was home.

"Yes, honey, what can I do for you?" I smiled.

"I love you," she said in a quiet voice, looking up at me earnestly.

I crouched down and hugged her closely. I could count on two hands the number of times Nadya had said "I love you" to me. "I love you too, sweetie."

She looked at me, eye to eye, as we stood in the kitchen. "Mom, I want to tell Dad I love him."

"Really?" I said, almost flabbergasted at the words coming out of her mouth.

"Yeah," she replied thoughtfully.

"Okay, well, let's go into the living room and you can tell him right now," I said. "Is that what you want?"

She nodded and asked me to come with her.

I took her by the hand and we walked over to Karl.

"Karl," I began, "Nadya has something she wants to say to you."

Karl muted the TV and looked at Nadya, who stood in front of him.

"What is it, Nads?" he inquired curiously.

"Nothing. I love you," she said quickly, almost with a shrug.

"Wow, thank you, Nads." Karl beamed. "I love you too, honey. I really do."

With that, Nadya and I walked back to the kitchen.

"Wow, Nadya," I encouraged her. "That was a really nice thing for you to say to Dad. I think you made him really happy."

She looked up at me and smiled. I could hardly believe this was the same girl that a year ago was running away from home, screaming, room wrecking, and abusing me. Karl and I made eye contact across the room. *She is getting better*, my eyes said, and I knew he felt the same way.

Later that day, Delaney was upset and yelled at me when I told her she couldn't sleep over at her friend's house, again.

"She should have a quiet room," Nadya whispered to me.

"That would be nice, wouldn't it?" I said, smiling at my oldest daughter's perceptiveness.

"I wish I had a quiet room here, too," she said.

"Well, you can always go to your room and listen to music with headphones," I reminded her.

"I know," she replied with a confident nod. "I like doing that."

We started seeing a beacon of light at the end of a dark tunnel our family had inhabited for years.

CHAPTER 14
TWO STEPS FORWARD, ONE STEP BACK

One of the other important developments during this time was that GLS was able to gradually decrease Nadya's medications. Since Texas, she had been on a "cocktail" of heavy anti-psychotic medications, many of them in adult dosages. GLS staff were able to decrease or eliminate most of the medication because it seemed that the structured, predictable, and calm environment was helping. She still remained on much smaller dosages of some medications that seemed to help take the edge off of her intense moods, but it was much less than before. Now that she understood she was in a safe and supportive place day in and day out, she was also more responsive to her caretakers, and more "available" for therapeutic changes that would positively rewire her brain, without mood-altering drugs interfering.

Despite all her progress, it wasn't always smooth sailing. While she didn't rage, scream, and throw things very often or for very long, she was still often defiant and oppositional for what seemed like no reason at all. One Sunday morning, we finished eating breakfast as a family and were putting on our coats to go to church. I ran out to the driveway to get the car warmed up, then headed back inside to finish getting ready. Karl always left thirty minutes before us because he volunteered to play drums and guitar in the church band, so it was up to me to get Delaney, Connor, and Nadya to the service.

"Nayda, honey!" I called from the bottom of the stairs. "Connor and Delaney are already waiting for us in the car. It's time to go!"

I had seen that she was already dressed and had her boots on, so I didn't know what was taking her so long. Finally, she emerged from her bedroom and stomped down the stairs, clearly in a foul mood, although I had no idea why. She had been fine at breakfast less than an hour earlier.

"Come on, honey, let's go; we're going to be late," I urged her. "Here's your jacket." I held it up for her to put on.

She crossed her arms over her chest and glared at me.

"What is it, Nadya?" I asked. "Don't you want to go to church and see your daddy playing the guitar? Just like we do every Sunday?"

She didn't respond. She just stood there looking at me.

"It'll be fun!" I tried using humor. "We can laugh at Dad when he makes silly faces at us when he's playing. Let's hurry up so we can get a good seat by him."

She grudgingly took the jacket and put it on, not saying a word.

"It's so cold outside, honey; zip up your coat."

She ignored me.

"Please, Nadya. I don't want you to get sick."

Nothing.

"Okay, well, just hurry up and get in the car. Connor and Delaney are waiting."

I hurried us outside and got in behind the wheel. Nadya stood beside the rear passenger door, refusing to get in.

"Man, what's her issue now?" said Connor, exasperated, from the front passenger seat.

"Shh, don't say anything. She'll be fine—just give her a minute," I replied. I rolled down the window a bit on Connor's side.

"Come on, honey, it's so cold out there. Get in so you don't freeze to death."

"No."

I knew that tone meant trouble. *Oh, God, no, no, please no*, I prayed. Nadya paced outside the car, jacket open, without a hat and gloves in the below-freezing temperatures of a Midwestern winter. I got out of the car and walked around to the other side to face her.

"Come on, honey," I said in my sweetest and calmest voice. "Church will be fun, remember? We'll get to sing songs and wave to Dad." I held the door open for her. "Ready?" I said with a big smile. "We don't want to be late."

Begrudgingly, she got in the car, and I closed the door behind her.

Whew, I thought. I got behind the wheel, backed down the driveway, and started hurrying down our street to church.

"Nadya, please put your seatbelt on, just like everybody else in the car," I said as I looked in the rearview mirror.

"No!" she yelled. My heart sank. "No! Stop the car!" she yelled again, kicking the seat.

"I can't stop the car right now, Nadya. I'm driving to church," I replied, hearing the anxiety in my own voice.

"Stop!" she yelled. "You do it!"

"I can't stop, honey. Not right now. I'll stop when we get to church. You know how to put your seatbelt on yourself. I don't have to stop the car for you to put it on."

I always walked a fine line between wanting to keep her safe and not wanting to push her into a rage. I was driving down the main street in our neighborhood to get to church, when suddenly, in one swift motion, Nadya flew between the two front seats and slammed my gear-shift into park.

The car came to an abrupt, grinding halt, a sickening sound of twisting metal coming from the engine as it shut off. We were all thrown violently forward in our seats, but Nadya managed to brace herself on the console. Delaney screamed at the top of her lungs.

"What the hell!" yelled Connor, and at the same time, Nadya began to scream.

If I had been going any faster than thirty miles per hour, or if there had been anyone behind us, I'm sure we would have gotten into a terrible accident. As it was, I sat there shaking with my hands on the wheel in the middle of the road. I tried to wrap my mind around what had just happened.

Okay, okay, get a grip, I repeated to myself. I looked in my rearview mirror to see if there were any cars coming up behind me. I turned the key in the ignition, praying it would turn over, and thankfully it did. I pulled over into a nearby neighborhood and stopped the car again.

"Is anybody hurt?" I asked urgently. "Delaney, Connor—are you guys okay?"

Delaney cried big, fearful tears, but she was just frightened by the abrupt stop and her screaming sister. Connor shook his head.

He inclined his head in Nadya's direction. "I'm fine, but she's crazy."

"Okay, you guys, just—just get out of the car. Walk home." I spoke to Connor and Delaney as I tried to articulate myself above Nadya's screams.

Delaney cried to me. "Mom, it's cold out! And I want to go to church!"

"I know, honey, but it's not far—only a little over a block away. I don't think we're going to make it to church today. Just hurry."

Connor threw his hands up in exasperation. "So we're not going to church now?" he fumed.

"No, I have to deal with this. Just please help your sister get home." And with that, the two of them exited the car and I watched them scurry down the sidewalk through the dusting of snow on the ground, huddled together against the cold.

I turned my attention to Nadya, who was in an all-out rage in the backseat now, red-faced, screaming, and kicking the seat as hard as she could.

"Nadya, it's okay," I began. "Please stop kicking the seat."

"No!" she continued to wail.

All I could do was pray to God for strength. *Here we are again*, the voice in my head was saying. *Here we are again.* I hated this. I was so afraid. I did not know what she would do next. What had set her off before we left? Was it that she didn't want to sit next to Delaney? Did she want to sit in the front? My mind was racing. I knew I had to be calm to get Nadya to be calm. I closed my eyes for a moment and drew in a few long, deep breaths. Regardless of all the practice I'd had with this over the years, I was scared to be in the car alone with her.

"Shh, it's okay, honey," I began again. "I'm not mad."

I didn't even look in her direction. I didn't try to make eye contact with her in the rearview mirror. I knew she didn't want me looking at her, and I was afraid to look at her anyway. When she was at a level five, I had to be as neutral, calm, and nonthreatening as possible. It was my only hope. I let her scream and kick some more, occasionally offering a few words of calm.

An hour passed. I knew Karl would be heading home from church soon, wondering what had happened to us. I hoped he had thought to call home to speak to Connor or Delaney. I could not use my phone in the car with Nadya acting out. If I got on the phone and said anything, it would enrage her more. Nadya was still screaming as I sat there, trying to offer soothing words in the pauses between her screams.

Just then, I saw a man walking his dog down the street in the distance.

"Oh, look, Nadya." I pointed to the sidewalk. "What kind of dog do you think that is?"

She quieted, looking curiously out the window. "There's a dog?" she asked, red-faced and tear-streaked.

"Yep . . . right there. See?" I said. "Walking towards us. I think maybe it's a chocolate Lab. What do you think?"

She looked intensely out the window, searching, and shortly, her eyes found the dog. It grabbed her attention, and I found my lifeline.

"Yeah, I think it's a Lab," she said tentatively.

"Do you think he's cold?" I asked.

"I don't know, maybe."

"Well, it looks like his tail is wagging."

"Yeah, his tail is wagging," she said, sounding assured.

"What does that mean when a dog's tail wags?" I asked.

"That means he's happy," she replied.

And so, for the next fifteen minutes we watched the man walk his dog down the street and back, and Nadya was completely captivated. She forgot what she had been raging about, and I started to calm down. By the time the man and the dog were out of sight, she was happy and cheerful, chatting with me from the backseat.

I turned to her now, finally.

"Now, Nadya, honey," I began gently, knowing she was finally receptive. "We need to talk about what just happened. It's very dangerous for you to touch the gearshift when I'm driving. You know that, right?"

She looked back at me with docile eyes.

"We all could have been really hurt, and our car could have been completely ruined," I explained in a soft voice. "I love you so much, and I don't want you to get hurt. I don't want Connor and Delaney to get hurt, either . . . that's why we all wear our seatbelts. Do you understand?"

She nodded. "I'm sorry," she said, and I was so relieved to hear those words—which I didn't hear often. It was a huge sign of progress from her.

"It's okay, honey." I smiled. "I'm not mad at you at all. I love you. Now, will you please put your seatbelt on so I can turn around and drive us home?"

She nodded and clicked her seatbelt, and just like that, we were back to normal and on our way home. Adrenaline still raced through my veins, as I learned the important lesson that despite all the improvements we saw in her, she was still fundamentally a traumatized child who would always need specialized care.

...

One of the most important aspects of the GLS program is that it gives families a respite. Because we had the full week to recover, we had more energy and emotional reserves to deal with Nadya's rages when they did happen on the weekends. We always knew that come Sunday night, she would go back to GLS, and we would go back to our peaceful home. When we didn't have all the built-up stress from a week of outbursts, we were much better able to handle what outbursts did happen on the weekends. The effect on Nadya was remarkable. When our child saw us in a relaxed state, she was more relaxed, and the positive cycle would build on itself. We always knew if things got too out of control, we could take her right back to GLS. A year into her stay, we had learned to trust the process, and knew that taking Nadya there for treatment was the best thing we had ever done for her. We knew the entire GLS staff was one hundred percent on our side, and so we felt good about dropping her off there every time. We knew they would know what to do—even when we felt like we didn't.

Nadya continued to come home for her weekend visits, and because they were so calm, we started extending them. She started staying home regularly for Sunday night as well, and Karl would drive her back to school Monday morning on his way to work. These visits got longer and longer, until Nadya was staying at home five nights a week, and only spending two nights at GLS. She wanted to stay home all the time, but she never argued too much when we told her she still had to live at the school part-time.

We contemplated putting her in a halfway house that was often the transition home for children coming out of residential care. It was basically a house where older children lived with supervision, but they had chores and jobs they had to do. They were expected to be much more self-sufficient. They had to do their own laundry, learn how to cook meals, and do the dishes. We battled back and forth with the pros and cons of her staying there. Decision-making about Nadya's future was always this way. It was always an emotional roller coaster—no decision was easy.

"She would learn how to do these important things that she needs to learn at some point," I said to Karl. "She doesn't do them at home, so maybe this would be a good way for her to learn."

Then the next day I would change my mind. "No, she really needs to come home," I said to Karl. "I'll teach her how to do laundry and things like that."

Karl agreed.

We decided we would spare her the move to the transition house, and just bring her home, which she wanted more than anything. By the time she had been in GLS for two years, the rages had completely stopped, although she occasionally exhibited resistance at home. Even then, her overall attitude was dramatically improved. We counted fourteen straight weekend visits without a single issue, and were floored at the progress she had made. We didn't want to risk any regression by putting her through another big transition, and we figured that we could handle her behavior on our own now. Plus, I missed her—I wanted her home. Delaney and Connor may have disagreed, but I had to do what I felt was right for Nadya.

Our family found itself once again faced with a challenging decision. Nadya had been at GLS for twenty-seven months—and for the past two-plus years, I had dedicated much of my attention to Connor and Delaney, who were both doing well in school and enjoying our peaceful family time. This was something I didn't want to change. It was so nice to be able to come home each day and just sit down to dinner with the kids, help Delaney with her homework, and not have to worry about any drama. I wondered if bringing Nadya home full-time meant more sacrifice for the other kids. I tossed and turned over the decision, my mind never really resting.

We could have hemmed and hawed over the decision for a long time, but at a certain point, Karl and I realized we just needed to choose, and then move forward with the courage and faith we had depended on from day one.

So in April 2013, we brought Nadya Hope Hetzel home for good.

CHAPTER 15
OUR BIGGEST FEAR

When we decided to bring Nadya home permanently, Ms. Jade and Nadya's special activities coordinator, Jennifer, were on hand to hug her and say goodbye. Jennifer had developed a particularly close relationship with Nadya over the past year. She was responsible for Nadya's free time—she helped Nadya prepare for the special Olympics, and was the person who would take Nadya off campus for her shopping trips and to get special treats. Jennifer hugged Nadya tightly as they said goodbye, tears filling both of their eyes. I was so proud to see that my daughter was showing emotion and vulnerability as she hugged Jennifer back.

We were all a little anxious, Delaney in particular, but the first few weeks were an incredible honeymoon period with Nadya at home. We got her enrolled right away in state-mandated follow-up care called the Wraparound Program. It provided an on-call crisis coordinator to help us manage urgent situations, as well as a mentor who visited the house three times a week to take Nadya on outings. We also met monthly with a representative from the Child Services Bureau who oversaw the support team we had in place and helped monitor Nadya's progress.

While it wasn't always a smooth process to assemble the right people around Nadya, and we went through several crisis coordinators and mentors before we found the right fit, we finally felt like we at least had a framework of support and tools at our disposal, and we were hopeful that the plan would work. It was very different from the period before GLS. The Wraparound Program, along with the long-term follow-up care program known as Reach, promised us a safety net.

We also started therapy with Dr. Wilson again, which Nadya enjoyed because she had always had a good connection with her. It also felt like we could make far more progress now because not only was Nadya much more verbal, but she had a better grasp on language and could talk about her feelings with us during the sessions.

The summer she spent at home was uneventful. Connor had just graduated high school but was still living at home, and the two of them were fine being home alone together during the day. Delaney had various activities like camp and summer school that kept her busy, but she was often home with the other two kids for the summer as well.

Things were relatively calm. But it was only the calm before the storm.

That fall, Nadya would be entering eighth grade at the local middle school, which she was actually excited about attending. We met with the staff ahead of time and they assured us they would have all the special education resources in place so that she started off on the right path. Everything seemed to be set up for success.

Nadya was excited for her first day of school, and

when the day in early September came, she got up and ready without a hitch. I was so grateful that she had made this much progress, and that I could count on her to get ready in the mornings like a normal teenager.

Within a few weeks, however, she started showing more resistance, locking herself in the bathroom for long periods of time and not listening to me. One day in early October, I went to wake the girls up as I always did.

"Good morning, girls!" I said as cheerfully as was possible at six thirty a.m. "Time to get ready for school." Delaney was already awake and getting out of bed. Nadya, however, looked up at me and then rolled over onto her other side.

That wasn't a good sign, but I backed out of the room and quietly closed the door, hoping she would pull herself out of it.

Five minutes later, I checked back in on her. She hadn't moved. This time, I went over to the bed, sat down on the edge, and put my hand on her shoulder.

"Nadya, honey," I began gently. "It's time to get up for school. Aren't you excited about eighth grade? Remember how excited you were just a few weeks ago?"

"No!" came the abrupt answer, and I flinched. This wasn't good. She threw back the covers, huffed at me as she flung her body out of bed, and stormed past me on her way to the bathroom, clothes in her arms. When Nadya realized the door was locked because Delaney was inside, she pounded the side of her fist on the door.

"Delaney!" she yelled.

"She'll be out in just a minute, honey," I said quickly as I walked up beside her. "Let her finish getting ready and then it will be your turn. Delaney, are you almost done?"

I called anxiously.

"Mom, I'm coming out right now," came Delaney's exasperated reply.

Nadya drew in a hardy breath and let out a scream—the first I had heard from her in a long time—and I froze, shocked. Fear rippled through my body, and the vibration of her shrill voice triggered the muscle memory I had of all her rages past, effectively paralyzing me where I stood.

At the shrieking, Delaney came out of the bathroom looking frantic and fearful. "Whoa, what was that?" Delaney said. "Geez," she added, looking at Nadya, who stood there, panting.

"Be quiet Delaney!" Nadya screamed, and pushed past her, storming in and locking the bathroom door behind her.

"Never mind . . ." I said in a quiet voice and gave Delaney a familiar look, which said *Be careful and don't push it right now.* The land mines were out.

"Delaney, honey, just go down and eat your breakfast," I managed to say with a dry throat.

"I knew this would happen again," Delaney said, as she headed toward the stairs. She turned and narrowed her eyes at me. "I hate her here."

"Delaney, please don't say that," I pleaded.

"It's true," she replied as she stood across from me in the hallway.

I fought my own disappointment to comfort Delaney. "Go eat your pancakes before they get cold. Everything is going to be fine."

"Yeah, sure it is," she replied sarcastically, and ran down the stairs.

I turned my attention back to the locked bathroom door.

"Nadya, honey," I began. "Are you okay in there?"

No answer.

"Don't forget to brush your teeth," I spoke in a quiet voice again. I heard her moving around in the bathroom, but no other sound emanated. After a minute of quiet, I returned to my bedroom downstairs to get ready. *Damn it!* The voice inside my head was so angry. *Why? Why? Why can't she just get ready? Why?* I sat on the bed, feeling sick.

"Mom!" Nadya screeched from within the bathroom, startling my nerves.

Stomp, stomp, stomp, I heard on the floor above me.

"I'm coming, Nadya," I yelled. I opened my bedroom door and made my way upstairs again. I still wasn't ready for work myself.

"What is it, honey?" I answered as I went back to her bathroom door.

But again, no answer came.

Nadya just wanted me to stand outside the bathroom while she took her time getting ready. I knew where this was going. This was how Nadya tried to control situations. It felt like manipulation, even though I knew she wasn't consciously trying to be malicious.

I relaxed my shoulders and replied as calmly as I could. "Honey, I have to go get ready too. Just hurry up and I'll see you downstairs for breakfast."

"No!" she shouted.

I didn't know what to do. I had to get ready for work. I couldn't stand outside the bathroom waiting for her all morning. I thought I would wait for just a few minutes to see if she came out, but just then Delaney came back upstairs.

"I need to brush my teeth, but my toothbrush is in there." She gestured to the locked bathroom door, and I took a deep breath before I called gently through the door to Nadya again.

"Honey, are you almost done? I don't want you to be late for the bus. Delaney needs to brush her teeth too, so hurry up and come out of there, okay?"

"No!" she shouted again.

I decided to switch gears and try something else. I put on my best British accent, pretending to be a character that Nadya had always loved. I cleared my throat very loudly.

"Excuse me, madam," I started in as though I were addressing the queen. "Is there a Miss Nadya Hetzel available? I have something I'd like to show her."

Silence on the other side. That was good—it meant she was listening.

I went on. "You see, we have found a certain item here which needs her immediate inspection. I keep hearing a strange whistling and I was wondering if she could tell me where it was coming from."

I had a special talent for whistling through my teeth like a ventriloquist, without pursing my lips, and it always made Nadya laugh. I hoped this would intrigue her. I heard the door unlock.

I breathed as quietly as I could and she opened the door a crack to look out at me; Delaney stood off to the side.

"Are you Miss Nadya Hetzel?" I inquired in British English.

She made eye contact with me. I touched her nose lightly with my pointer finger and whistled through my teeth.

"You see, I've heard you have a nose that whistles, and I'm very curious about it."

I very carefully lifted my finger to her nose and whistled again . . . and she laughed.

"Yes, just as I suspected—you have a magic nose, you little stinker!" Even Delaney couldn't help smiling at my accent as she watched from the hallway.

"My nose doesn't whistle," Nadya giggled.

"Well, it would appear that it does," I said, pushing and whistling again. "How funny it is indeed—it's true. Nadya Hetzel has a nose that whistles." I pushed and whistled her nose again.

My ventriloquist act had refocused her, diffusing a rapidly escalating situation. Humor didn't always work—I had to catch her before she really got angry, but we were safe, for now. The girls finished getting ready and headed to school. I had to hurry up and wash my face and apply what makeup I could and head out the door to get to work on time. I had stopped working for the adoption agency not too long after we brought Nadya home, and I had recently gone back to work in a dentist's office. Once I got there, I had to switch it on and be ready to make children's visits to the dentist fun. Inside, my brain and body were recovering from the events of the morning, which had left me shaky.

Soon, it became clear that the transition into eighth grade was not going well for Nadya. She started resisting me every day. Sometimes I was able to calm her down before she blew up, but finally there came the day when

I couldn't, and she turned violent—an old-fashioned Nadya rage just like in the years before GLS. I had to call the police, and I felt the terrible sinking feeling that my life was returning to the fear I had known before. In much the same way they had so many times before, I needed the police to help me settle Nadya down because she was screaming at me, refusing to do what was asked of her, and slamming the bathroom door in my face whenever I approached her. Nadya threw things at me when I was calling 911 and then she hid behind a couch until things were settled down and the police were gone. Our unwelcome guest, the Big Fear, was back.

By mid-October, I had already called 911 twice in the mornings. The crisis coordinators provided by the Wraparound Program never made it to the house in time to help with an escalating situation, and of course when they were there, Nadya never raged—so it seemed they didn't believe I was having issues with her. I felt myself spiraling again, quickly returning to high levels of stress. I once again had trouble sleeping, and was in a continual tug of war with both girls. Delaney began having problems in school, and I felt I was to blame.

One morning in late October, we made it as far as breakfast with only resistance and opposition, but once I asked Nadya to sit down at the table to eat her cereal and take her pills, she exploded. I wasn't sure what set her off. I asked Delaney if she'd said anything to her sister and she said no. Nadya glared at Delaney and me and began throwing things and kicking me whenever I got near her. There seemed to be nothing I could do to calm her down.

"Please, Nadya, come on. Settle down," I pleaded with her. "You're scaring Zoe."

Zoe was barking and going after her ankles. I tried to pick the dog up, but Nadya got mad and started to grab at her. Zoe was struggling to get out of my arms, and I quickly put her in my bedroom and closed the door. Nadya ran to my room to try to let the dog out.

"Nadya! Stop it," I said sternly. "Leave the dog alone." Nadya only wanted the dog out to aggravate me.

"You can't make me!" she yelled, her grip firmly on the knob. Zoe was barking loudly behind the door.

"Nadya, just get your shoes on and get ready for the bus," I said as coolly as possible, but my insides were quaking. She kept her hand on the door and her eyes on me, refusing to move.

"Nadya, the dog stays there. She is scared," I said firmly. I maneuvered myself in between her and the doorknob and made her move away. She kicked me. Then she went into the kitchen and scanned the room methodically for things to launch at me before running back to the bedroom door to let the dog out.

"No!" I yelled. "Get ready for school right now, Nadya!" How I wished Karl could be there to help, but he usually left for work before we got up.

She went to the bathroom and picked up a heavy ceramic soap dish and, with all her might, threw it at my head. I ducked, and it hit my shoulder and shattered on the ground.

I didn't know how much more of this I could take. I was afraid, and so was Delaney.

We had learned long ago to move the knives and glasses up higher where Nadya couldn't reach them, but I did a quick sweep with my eyes just to make sure there was nothing truly dangerous within her reach.

I tried ignoring her and going about my business getting breakfast ready for Delaney, but as soon as I turned my back on Nadya, she got in front of my face and screamed even louder. She slammed one kitchen chair after another down to the floor until the kitchen looked like a tornado had hit it. I handed Delaney her bowl of oatmeal and told her to go eat in her room.

"She can't eat in her room!" screamed Nadya, and Delaney knew better than to respond. She slid her way up the stairs as quickly as possible, leaving her oatmeal at the table.

Nadya ran over to the large, fifty-two-inch flat-screen TV in the living room and grabbed the corner of it—looking at me to make sure I was watching. She started shaking the edge, as though she were threatening to bring it crashing down. I had already tried to restrain her that morning, wrapping my arms around her chest from behind and trying to remove from her hands the candles she wanted to throw. I had two big black bite-mark indentations on my forearm, almost overlapping, from where she had bitten me twice. They were already swelling into golf ball–sized lumps. She had also kicked me and spit in my face as I tried to get close to her.

Exhausted, I sat down on the couch.

"You could be really hurt if you knock that TV down," I said calmly. I tried to maintain a relaxed posture, pretending to be uninterested in the fact that Nadya was threatening to bring our expensive TV crashing to the ground.

"Go ahead," I said. "But you could get really hurt, and then you won't be able to watch TV anymore."

I had called and paged her crisis coordinator several

times earlier that morning and left messages asking her to please come as soon as possible, but hadn't heard back from her yet. *Where are these damn support people when you need them?* I thought.

Nadya shook the corner of the TV, breathing hard and looking at me with eyes that said *I'm going to knock it over, I'm going to knock it over. Just you watch.*

"Throw it on the floor, for all I care," I said again. I hoped my reverse psychology would work on her. "But just remember—no more TV for you then." I realized only too late that telling Nadya she wouldn't be able to watch TV anymore would only infuriate her further.

Nadya grabbed one of the remote controls lying on the TV stand and threw it at me. I stood up quickly and grabbed her hand as she reached down for the second remote. My body felt as if it were being swallowed up in quicksand. At that instant, she swung toward me with her closed right fist, cracking me just under my left eye. I let go of her hand, recoiling with a shock. Nadya was almost fifteen years old now and had a lot more strength than the nine-year-old we had brought home from Russia. Dazed and seeing stars, I stumbled back a few steps and sat down abruptly on the floor, bringing my hands up to my face. Nadya got up screaming and ran down the hall, oblivious to the pain she had just inflicted on me.

"Oh, no! Mommy are you okay?" yelled Delaney. She had seen what had happened and she was terrified. I was feeling unsteady and not seeing straight—my face started throbbing and I didn't feel like I could open my eye.

"Call 911," I said to Delaney through a fog. "Call 911, hurry." Delaney ran to grab the phone, and Nadya saw what she was doing. She started to scream at Delaney and made a beeline for her. I gathered myself enough to stand up and wrap my arms around Nadya, pulling her down to the couch as she tried to run past me toward Delaney. I twisted her pant leg as tight as I could around one leg to hold her down, and pressed into her body with mine to pin her to the edge of the couch. She resisted with all her might.

From the kitchen, I could hear Delaney urging the 911 operator to come quickly because her sister was attacking her mom. She ran back over to me when she was done.

"I called 911, Mommy, they're on their way," she cried to me from a safe distance as I held firmly to Nadya's pant leg.

"*Let me go! Let me go!*" Nadya screamed again and again.

"Thanks, Delaney. Now go—go, honey," I urged her, barely able to concentrate on her face. "I hear your bus coming; hurry up and get outside."

"I don't want to leave you!" she cried. "Mama—"

"I'll be fine. The police will be here in a minute, and I'm sure our stabilizer will show up, too. I'll be okay—you need to get to school. The police will be here soon. Go, please. I'll come check in on you at school when this is over."

I was numb and simultaneously overflowing with emotion—fear, anger, adrenaline, and sadness at seeing the terror reflected in Delaney's face. Things had been so good for over two years, and now just a few months after Nadya returned, things seemed worse than they ever had been.

Five minutes later, the police arrived. I released my

hold on Nadya, and she ran to the bathroom and slammed and locked the door. These were new officers who didn't know Nadya, but they immediately saw the bite marks on my arm and my rapidly swelling eye. I could already barely see out of it.

The police looked around the house at the mayhem—overturned chairs, broken pieces of ceramic from the soap dish, a hole in the wall from where one of the kitchen chairs had hit it, and the TV askew on the stand.

I went through the usual routine—explained that my daughter had RAD, and that she was adopted from Russia.

I sat on the couch across from the officers and sobbed. "I can't take this anymore, I just can't take this anymore," I kept repeating. I was in a state of shock, staring at the bite marks on my forearm. I could clearly make out her teeth.

"We can't leave you with her, ma'am," said one of the officers. "We need to make sure you are safe."

"You need to get some ice on your eye, too," said the other. By the way they looked at me—and from what I'd been through—I could tell I was a mess.

The officers stayed at the house for another hour, talking through the bathroom door to Nadya in a calm and friendly manner. Our crisis stabilizer finally arrived and asked what had happened, but I was still too shaken up to tell her. She, too, went to the bathroom door to try to talk to Nadya, and Nadya finally opened the door and let her in. I peeked in to see if I was able to come inside. Our crisis stabilizer nodded. Nadya sat on the toilet seat and started to come out of the haze of her rage. She looked at me remorsefully with tears running down her cheeks.

Whenever I saw her crying real tears, I saw it as a sign of her healing—a sign of her increasing ability to be vulnerable and present with her emotions. But it didn't make my injuries, emotional and physical, any less painful.

As difficult as it was, I knew I had to move in and comfort her. I looked at her with my one good eye and rubbed her shoulders, telling her I loved her and that it was okay.

"I'm sorry, Mama," she said in a whisper, barely looking at me through her tears. She didn't want to look at my eye or my arm.

"It's okay, honey. I know you are. I know you didn't mean to do it." It felt like I was going through the motions of my life—saying words I knew I needed to say, but barely feeling anything as the shock of the physical trauma reverberated throughout my body.

"We just had a bad morning, didn't we?" I said quietly. "Is it okay if I hug you?"

She gave a small nod. I pulled her to me and she sobbed. I held her like that for several minutes as she cried, eyes shut tightly, face pressed against my chest.

"Shhhh. You okay now, sweetie?" I asked, leaning back to look in her eyes. "We've got to get you to school." With that, we slowly stood up and finished getting dressed. In the meantime, I went to the bathroom to try to put myself together. My eye was too swollen and painful to put any makeup on. I couldn't go in to work looking like this—I would terrify the children as I was leaning over them to clean their teeth; and besides, I could barely think straight, let alone perform at work today. So I called in sick.

One of the officers stayed behind to make certain that things were stable. He opened the front door and Nadya saw that the police car was a Dodge Charger.

"You drive a Charger?" she asked, wide-eyed.

"Yes, our new cars are Chargers. Do you like them?"

Nadya was beaming. "Can you drive me to school?" she asked.

The officer looked at me for approval.

"Sure, why not?" I said. "Follow me, I'll lead the way," I told the officer. Once we arrived at school, Nadya got out of the car with a smile on her face.

"That is a cool car, Mom!"

The officer told Nadya to have a good day.

"Nadya, what do you say to him?" I reminded her.

"Thanks for the ride in your Charger!" she said enthusiastically to the officer, who gave her a wave and drove away.

I walked Nadya into the school and asked the receptionist to inform Nadya's teacher she was here. I also asked to speak with the dean of students. Nadya's teacher came to the lobby with a smile on her face, happy to see that Nadya had made it to school. Then she glanced up to me and her expression changed.

"Nadya is ready," I told her, weary but proud that she had made it out of her rage and could function normally just a short time later. Her teacher took Nadya's backpack and led her out of the office. "I'll see you in a little while, Nadya. Have a good rest of your day," I called after her, and she gave me a wave as she walked away with her teacher.

The dean of students showed me to his office, and I took a seat on the leather chair near his desk. His eyes widened and he pulled back, shocked by what he saw. He pushed the Kleenex box to me and I wiped my tears.

"Mrs. Hetzel, I am so sorry you have to go through this," he said. I tried to catch my breath, but it choked me. I could not stop crying.

"Can you please call Delaney out from her classroom?" I asked him. "She saw everything that happened this morning and I just want to assure her I'm safe." While in the office, I called Karl on my cell and told him to come home.

"What's going on, Lori?" he asked.

"Just come home. I need you," was all I could muster between sobs.

"Okay, I'm leaving now," he said, no questions asked. The man was a saint, and my savior. I knew I could count on his support when I got home.

Within a few minutes, Delaney came running into the office, bursting into tears when she saw me. She rushed over and put her arms around me, burying her face in my chest.

"Oh, Mommy, I was so worried! So scared!" she sobbed into my shirt. I could barely keep my own emotions from boiling over, but I maintained my composure. The dean excused himself and gave us some privacy.

"I hate her, Mommy," said Delaney. "I hate her so much for doing this to you."

"Shh, don't say that, honey," I said. "I know it's hard to see, but you don't hate her. She doesn't know what she is doing—she didn't mean to hurt me."

But the truth was that things between Delaney and Nadya would never be the same again—Delaney was traumatized by the violence she had seen in our home that morning, and from that point on, she would be on edge in a way she hadn't been before.

When Karl came home, I told him the full story. He just held me while I cried.

"Why didn't you call me right away?" he asked.

"I don't know, I didn't have time to," was all I could muster. "It all happened so fast."

I was so relieved that he was home that I fell asleep next to him on the couch until the girls came home from school.

That night, I ordered pizza. I could not bring myself to make anything for dinner. Everyone was tense, the whole family aware of the wounds on my arms and face. Nadya came slowly to the table and sat down next to me. I was worried that Delaney would give her a dirty look, but she kept her face down while eating her pizza.

Connor threw down his fork and turned on her. "Look at what you did to her!" he yelled at Nadya, furious.

"Connor, don't start with her," I said. "Please, we already took care of this. I don't need a repeat, got it?"

"No, someone needs to say it," he said, his face red and full of anger. "Look what you did to Mom! You don't deserve to have a mom like her!"

"Connor," Karl said. "Eat and don't say anything else."

"Connor," I said quietly, "just eat and please leave it alone. She said she was sorry. It was a very rough and long day for me. I need to relax."

He glared at Nadya for a moment longer before turning to me, exhaling. "Sorry, Mom," he said, and got up and gave me a hug. I reminded him that he held a special place in my heart. Logan was still at work and did not know what had taken place that day. Once again, I felt I was just barely able to hold my family together.

With her half-eaten pizza, Nadya got up from the

table and went to the couch, covering up with her blanket. Delaney shoved her pizza down to get away from the table and went upstairs to her room.

That night, I called the attorney who had represented us in the state proceedings and told him what had happened.

"We need to put her back in GLS full-time," I pleaded. "Please, there has to be something you can do. I'm not safe at home."

He was sympathetic, but of course I knew it wouldn't be that easy. He told me I was welcome to file another petition with the state to have her institutionalized again, but that the chances of her being sent to GLS were slim. If the judge thought her behavior was escalating, they would probably send her somewhere else. She could even end up in foster care. It was a chance I didn't want to take.

I didn't understand why this was happening—why was she regressing? Things had been so good for so long. She had been thriving at GLS and doing so well on her weekend visits with the family. I knew the transition back home and to a new school would be difficult for her, but this level of violence was completely unprecedented, even for Nadya. At this point, I had no idea what the future held.

CHAPTER 16
MOMENT OF TRUTH

The stress was truly reaching unbearable levels for me again. During a regular visit with my doctor, I asked for more anti-anxiety medications, and also told him about some troubling symptoms I had been having lately: episodes of confusion, forgetfulness, dizziness, and nausea. A few times, I had left my car running in the driveway after I parked at home, I had gotten lost on my way to work, and I had gotten lost at the office while escorting a child back for her cleaning. These periods of disorientation were frightening me. He referred me to a neurologist and I had an MRI. It turned out I had developed a form of non-convulsive epilepsy.

"Could this be brought on by stress?" I asked the neurologist when he told me that my brain showed definite signs of seizures over the past two months.

"Definitely," he said. "Have you had any particularly stressful incidents in your life lately?" he inquired innocently.

I sighed and pursed my lips. "Yes, you could say that." I decided there wasn't enough time in the day to explain Nadya to him. I was put on medication for the epilepsy, and the seizures seemed to lessen.

"You need to try to find ways to eliminate the stressors in your life," the doctor explained during a follow-up visit. *Hmm*, I thought. *Sure thing, doc*. If he only knew the full scope of the daily stress in my life, he'd probably have a seizure himself!

Meanwhile, I confided in Dr. Wilson about how worried I was that Nadya was regressing—that we were losing all the progress she had made during twenty-seven months at GLS.

She nodded thoughtfully. "It's really hard to reverse these neurological habits, Lori. You're experiencing that firsthand. The brain is an experience-dependent organ, and when there was all that stress during Nadya's important early developmental periods, it became a neurological habit for her brain to say, 'Okay, I'd better be ready to respond to stress because my environment has taught me that's what I need to do.' Even though we've taken her out of that stressful environment, we are still working on unwiring that neurological habit—and it takes a long time."

I always appreciated the way Dr. Wilson was able to calmly give me perspective on what was happening.

"It doesn't necessarily mean she's forgotten everything she learned at GLS," she continued. "But just like it's a neurological habit for me to write with my right hand—it would be extremely difficult for me to rewire my brain later in life to write with the left one, especially in times of urgency—the brain's default is to go back immediately to what's familiar. In Nadya's case, that's having a high reactivity to stress."

It made me feel better to understand that it wasn't

necessarily that we were losing all the progress we had made at GLS, but just that we had to focus on helping Nadya continue rewiring her brain with the positive new stress-response habits she'd developed there.

A few weeks later, we had our monthly team meeting at the school to discuss Nadya's education and progress (or the lack thereof) since our last meeting. Her teacher, along with our team from the Wraparound Program, Nadya's two unreliable crisis stabilizers, and the program coordinator, Lisa, were all present.

"Let's start with you, Lori," began the crisis coordinator. I cringed. I always felt I was being interrogated in these meetings. "Can you give us some feedback on positive improvements you've seen in Nadya's behavior since our last meeting?"

The whole long table of people turned to look at me, and I felt as though absolutely everything that was bad in Nadya's behavior was my fault, that it was caused by some lack of parenting expertise on my part.

"Well, she took a shower without me having to tell her ten times this week," I began. "And she got a perfect score on her spelling test." I was livid for what I felt was the presumptuous nature of these people. But I played their game.

"Oh, yes, Nadya is doing wonderful in school," chimed in Nadya's teacher with a smile.

Everyone nodded in happy agreement. I wrung my hands in my lap as everyone went around the room talking about how great Nadya was doing.

"Yeah, I never see any issues either," chimed in Ivana, one of our crisis stabilizers. "She's always calm and cooperative when I'm at the house."

I'd had enough. "No, listen, it's not as easy as you people think it is," I began angrily. "You don't understand—we live through hell at home. She rages and bites and kicks—our house is completely terrorized because of her behavior.

"What is the plan here?" I continued. "What, are we just going to go around and around again talking about how great she is doing when nothing ever gets done? Nothing is different; her behaviors are still awful—she is oppositional and defiant and violent. Yeah, she has some good days, but I just had a black eye last month, see?" I shouted, pointing to the fading green spots under my eye. "I lost three days of work, unpaid! I'm sick of it. I'm sick of it!" I fumed, and waited for a response. Everyone shifted uncomfortably, but no one said anything.

Then Lisa, Nadya's court-appointed caseworker, turned to me.

"But she seems to be doing so well," she said, not hearing a word I said.

I was on my feet now, standing at the end of the long table. "I've had it! I've had it with little Miss Nadya," I went on. "You can take her right back to f-ing court. Take her, because I have had it. I have had it. I am sick of being kicked, I am sick of being not listened to, I am sick of dealing with her every single morning." Tears fell uncontrolled from my eyes as my body shook. I had finally hit my limit. "Get out of the bathroom, Nadya, get out of the bathroom, Nadya, get out of the car, Nadya, get in the car, Nadya," I repeated. "I am sick of it!"

"Please, Lori, just sit down," said Lisa. "You don't really mean that."

"None of you people have kids," I interrupted her,

looking around at the team of mostly young people be-fore me. "You all work in the system and for the sys-tem, but you don't live in the system twenty-four-seven. I have had it. I am done. I wash my hands of this girl. I am done."

What I wanted more than anything was to be heard, for them to feel my frustration—for the team to *do something* to help our ailing family. Of course Nadya didn't act up around any of them. That was the nature of her disorder. How did they not understand that? I needed their support, not their finger pointing at me like I was crazy, making it up, or exaggerating.

"Well, your permanency plan will end in August, and you will legally reclaim all your full rights to Nadya as her parents. She will be your daughter again," explained Lisa.

I looked at her with incredulity on my face and a voice full of disgust. "Are you f-ing nuts?" *She doesn't get it,* I thought. *I love this girl and I'm losing my mind.* I needed their help! How could I get through?

"Of course we are Nadya's parents . . . we were always Nadya's parents! We went to Russia twice, and on the second trip, a Russian court said we became her parents and we have been since then and always will be."

"You guys have no idea what it's like," Karl added. "Lori has been taking abuse for six years. Six years! Can you even imagine that?"

I stood up and brought my hand down hard on the table. "I'm leaving," I declared. "Excuse me for my lan-guage. I know you're just trying to do your jobs, but I have to leave." I stormed out, leaving Karl to deal with them.

At home, I locked myself in the bedroom and bawled my eyes out as I drank a tall glass of wine. I felt embarrassed by my behavior and guilty for the things I had said.

Karl and I faced each other over the dinner table that night, feeling totally alone. We were surrounded by people who had only partial pictures of the state our family was in, and few ideas of how to offer us any support. It felt like a big game of hot potato.

I didn't really want to send Nadya away, I realized. I had hit a wall and just wanted her to be better. I wanted to be understood. I hadn't meant those horrible things, but I couldn't keep my frustration and pain in any longer. The cloud of despair hovered ever closer to me.

That summer when school ended, Delaney didn't want to go away to summer camp—an activity she used to love.

"Mommy, I'm so scared of leaving you alone with Nadya," she said to me. She wrapped her arms around me and hugged me like she never wanted to let go.

"It's okay, honey," I said. "Nadya was really sorry about what she did, and it won't happen again." But I knew that like me, Delaney wasn't convinced. We had all seen too much of Nadya's unpredictable behavior to feel much confidence one way or the other.

I was so tired of the roller coaster—tired of feeling hated and abused by the one I poured my heart and soul into. I wished she could learn to ask for things instead of demanding things. I wished I didn't have to tiptoe around my own house. I longed for what our family had been before Nadya returned home—sometimes I felt like the depths of madness were enveloping me and I couldn't see out of the darkness that threatened to swallow me up so wholly.

And yet, this girl could laugh with me, sit on my lap and cuddle sweetly on family movie nights. She loved watching Keith Urban videos with me. It wasn't all doom and gloom—Nadya had learned specific skills at GLS. I remember watching her in her classroom while she sat next to an autistic boy. There was a music stand behind the boy, which he knocked over in a sudden outburst, papers flying everywhere. He jumped up and covered his ears, panicked. I was so surprised when Nadya got out of her chair and calmly started picking up the papers for him.

"It's okay," she said to him simply.

As I watched her, I repeated to myself, *It is okay. It is. It is all right.*

The teacher commented on how nice it was for her to be helpful. And I was proud of her too, because just like Nadya, I was sure the boy didn't have any friends, either. I think Nadya was used to children having outbursts like that from her time at GLS, and she recognized that that boy was someone who was like her in a way. It was touching to see how calm and loving my daughter could be at times—she had come such a long way thanks to all the lessons she'd learned at GLS.

Sometimes, I truly saw glimpses of how far she had come. She didn't say she loved me, but I could tell she did because she always wanted extra hugs and squeezes. I didn't need words for that. I had to remind myself, too, that I wasn't the only one doing the hard work. Her emotions took her to places she didn't know how to respond to, and she was constantly trying to learn new ways of coping with them.

She could be very tenderhearted, too. When I was sick with a fever and lying on the couch, she tried in earnest to take care of me.

"Oh, Mama, your cheek is so hot!" she said as she laid her hand gently on my face. "You must not feel good!" She ran and got me a glass of water and covered me up with a blanket. Those moments were precious to me.

That summer, we were assigned a new mentor for Nadya. Emily was a lovely young gal and Nadya took a liking to her. She would come by on Wednesdays and Fridays to get Nadya out of the house for a few hours. She had signed Nadya up to volunteer at one of our local pet stores, so on Wednesdays, Nadya and Emily would walk the puppies outside. Nadya absolutely loved it, and we knew that if we had any issues on any given day, we could rely on Emily to help. I had Mondays off work, so I tried to be with her while Delaney swam at the nearby park pool. Tuesdays, Thursdays, and alternating Fridays, Nadya would stay home alone and watch TV on the couch. Connor would be at home for a while before heading to work in the afternoons, so if there were any problems, he could call me. Luckily, Nadya always did fine by herself at home with Zoe, our dog. She and Connor pretty much left each other alone.

...

When I didn't have to get her up for school in the mornings, she didn't rage, and thankfully, the summer passed uneventfully. In the fall, however, she had to start another new school—high school—and our family was once again terrified at what it would bring.

All summer long, Karl and I experienced peak anxiety

levels because we didn't think she would agree to get up and go to school the day after Labor Day, no matter how much we tried to prepare her.

I redoubled my efforts to be the mother this little girl needed. She still didn't truly understand the concept of a mother, and it was up to me to teach her what a mother is. I wanted her to trust me and feel safe with me. I wanted her to see that I would never give up. I wanted to teach her how love felt, what love is. I wanted to show her compassion and understanding. I wanted to be her mother.

I had so often thought of loving harder. Loving harder is the hardest thing I have ever done. To me it was like climbing Mount Everest—just when I thought I had taken two steps upwards, I slipped back down a jagged piece of ice. There were moments when I was defeated and lower than I had been before, but I was determined to love this girl, no matter what.

CHAPTER 17
FACING THE FUTURE

We had worked together with Nadya's eighth-grade teachers to put a plan in place for her transition to high school the following year—even though we still weren't completely sure we were going to send her there. The truth was that Karl and I had debated long and hard about whether to even start Nadya in high school, or if she should just repeat eighth grade. She had developed an especially tight bond with one of the teachers there, which was rare and which we knew would be hard for her to leave behind. We dreaded putting her through another rough transition when she had just gotten used to middle school. But Mrs. Harding, one of the aides that worked with Nadya in eighth grade, would be working at the high school with Nadya as well, and that seemed to ease some of Nadya's fears. In the middle of eighth grade, we'd started taking Nadya to the high school every day for a few hours so she could familiarize herself with the layout. Mrs. Harding would meet us in the lobby and walk Nadya to her classrooms, and Nadya participated in an art club there in the late afternoons.

"Mama, I don't want to go to that school," she told me

often. "I'm afraid." She was scared of how big the school was.

"You know, Nadya, you will spend most of your day down here," her special education teacher explained while we were visiting one day with Mrs. Harding. "You will only have to go to gym, music, and your special reading class. You'll always have someone with you so you don't get lost."

Nadya nodded as if she understood, but her face revealed her confusion. We kept stressing to her how well she was going to know the school by the time freshman year rolled around in a few months, and that Delaney wouldn't know the school at all. That seemed to make her feel better.

Even so, the entire summer before high school was to begin, Karl and I were still on the fence about which option to choose. The only real alternative besides the local high school was to send her to the Sawyer House—a type of halfway home for older teens who were transitioning out of the Genesee Lake School residential program. Sawyer House usually had five to seven special needs girls like Nadya living together along with a small team of trained staff. Sawyer House was the one we visited before deciding to bring Nadya home for good. The home was well run and successful for many older students. The biggest problem was that she didn't want to go there—at all. She wanted to come home. At that time, her aversion to the Sawyer House seemed greater than her resistance to the high school.

In addition, I was also worried that she wouldn't be able to handle the increased responsibilities she would be required to have at the Sawyer House—namely, having chores like doing her own laundry, preparing simple meals (even if it just meant microwaving them), and cleaning up after herself. Nadya had never been able to do any of these things, and because she was making so much progress when her time at GLS was ending, I thought I would be able to teach her these things on my own, at home.

What's more, enrollment at the Sawyer House would require us to involve the courts again, and I wasn't sure I wanted to go down that route. It wouldn't have been a sure thing anyway, getting the state to agree to send her there and pay for it. The funding for mental health care in our state had been steadily dwindling in recent years, and the Mental Health Complex at the hospital would soon be closing. I thought of all the children and adults who relied on those state services, and wondered where they were going to go after the funds dried up.

"We'll make it work," I told Karl, although in hindsight I wish we had sent her to the Sawyer House.

It wasn't until we had a meeting with her entire special education team at the high school in August that we decided to enroll her in high school. Dr. Wilson was a huge help to us in getting Nadya psychologically ready for the transition. In therapy, Dr. Wilson helped Nadya understand that it was okay to say goodbye to her beloved eighth-grade teacher. The fact that she was able to recognize that he was important to her—and express sadness about it without getting angry—was a huge step forward in her progress. That Nadya felt safe enough with those sad feelings to let them show, rather than masking them behind anger, was one of the first times in her life that she was able to display such emotional maturity.

Additionally, Dr. Wilson pointed out that Nadya was able to repair herself in a way that none of us were sure was possible. In the weeks after Nadya had given me the black eye, we were able to revisit that trauma during therapy. Dr. Wilson had printed out pictures of my bruises, bite marks, and black eye, and we went over them in one of our sessions. Nadya sat forward in her chair and looked at the pictures, understanding that she had done that to me. It was hard for her to see me hurt, and it made her sad. But she allowed herself to feel those uncomfortable emotions instead of getting angry—which was something she had never done in years of therapy. She was able to express to me how sorry she was that she had hurt me, which helped solidify for her the idea that all relationships have ruptures and tension, but that we can repair that damage. This alone was a hugely valuable lesson, and it had taken years to sink in with her. There was so much to be hopeful about.

Despite all the hardships and increased violence at home during her eighth-grade year, the summer after school let out led to some of the best family times we had ever had. It had been just over a year since Nadya left GLS, and we decided we would plan our first-ever family vacation. We wanted to take Delaney to visit the water parks in Wisconsin Dells, but taking Nadya there on a day trip years ago had resulted in a meltdown so horrendous that we had not attempted another family vacation in the five years since. The park was loud and noisy, full of people and unpredictable situations—a field of land mine triggers for Nadya's rage. However, after failing to find a suitable place for Nadya to stay for the weekend, we decided to take her with us. We all needed a break—some fun time. Delaney deserved it.

Weeks in advance, I showed Nadya pictures of the hotel and the water park, and explained to her that it would be loud and there would be a lot of people.

"This is our hotel where we'll be staying. It looks like a log cabin—isn't that neat?" I flipped through a brochure of the hotel with Nadya on my lap. "They have an arcade and a pool, so many places to play and have fun." I kept stressing how the point of all of this was to have *fun*— that that is what family vacations are for—but I knew she didn't completely understand. After all, she had never truly experienced "family fun" before.

"Lots of families go there to have fun," I told her again and again. "There will be a lot of noise and activity, but there is no yelling or screaming. If you need to come out of the water or when I have to tell you it's time to go back to the hotel, that's not part of the family fun time." I built the trip up so much for Nadya that she was actually excited to go. Delaney, on the other hand, was skeptical about having her along.

When the time came, we set off with trepidation, and it started well when the girls each happily played on their iPods and iPads in the backseat for the whole hour-and-a-half drive. Surprising all of us, Nadya went out of her comfort zone willingly, going down a few slides and spending several hours each day floating on the lazy river. She didn't give us a lick of trouble or defiance the entire weekend. She got ready to go when it was time, left the park when we were done, and was quiet and respectful at meals in loud restaurants, even when other children were running around screaming. My heart beamed with pride for how far she had come.

In the end, I was beyond surprised by how much fun our family had on that trip—even though the boys weren't with us. Everyone got along, and it was a completely stress-free weekend. It was some of the first truly happy time we had together, and I was so glad that our family could finally develop some treasured memories. I realized once again that despite all I had been through, I still needed to give this little girl a chance. She still had the capacity to surprise me.

When we returned home, though, Karl's and my anxiety rose the closer we got to Labor Day, after which we would need to wake her up for high school. I shook just thinking about some of the hellish mornings I'd had with her last year.

Once again, though, my girl managed to surprise me.

"You did it again!" I exclaimed with joy as I walked into the kitchen and found her sitting there, dressed and ready for the day during the second week of school. I poured her a bowl of cereal and gave her some juice.

"I'm so proud of you!" I beamed.

She looked puzzled.

"Nadya, do you know that since the first day of school, you have been the first one up and ready to go every day?"

"I am?" she asked.

"Yes, you are!"

She smiled, then dipped her spoon into her bowl of cereal and gulped it down. Once the bowl was empty, she looked up at me.

"I already took my pills, too," she added with a quick shrug.

"I'm so impressed, Nads!"

She knew that when she was up and ready early, she

would be allowed to play on my tablet and get a piece of gum—two of her favorite treats.

I was encouraged by her willingness to give the new school a try. I thought maybe she could successfully complete her four years there, even though she would be twenty-one when she graduated. We knew the following year, when she turned seventeen, we would have to take legal guardianship of her. We had to ensure that in all legal matters for the rest of her life—finances, health, and so forth—we would be able to be in control. She was not capable of making her own decisions in any capacity, and we would always have to be responsible for her. For as long as we lived, we would be Nadya's legal guardians. In all my life, I never thought I would need to be my child's permanent guardian. I just wanted to be her parent, her mom.

While Nadya behaved when it came to school, she started acting out in other ways. As soon as she got home each afternoon, she became lethargic and refused to do anything at all. At first, I thought she was just worn out from her day at school. But every night, when I told Nadya that she needed to take a shower and put her jammies on, she resisted.

"You can't make me. It's not Sunday."

"I know it's not Sunday, Nadya, but at Genesee Lake School you had to take a shower every night, remember? I'm only telling you to take one at least three times a week."

"I'm not doing it," she replied, and turned away from me.

"Nadya, your hair is really dirty and your body needs to be washed," I pleaded.

She silently refused to acknowledge me.

We had worked with Dr. Wilson to come up with a list of activities that Nadya enjoyed, and she had agreed to do two of them on Saturday and two on Sunday. We needed this system in place just to get her out of the chair. The list included things like playing in the backyard for twenty minutes or riding her bike. I told her she just needed fresh air and exercise—that she could sit on the porch with me for twenty minutes to soak in the sunshine and that could count as one of her activities that day. While she agreed to them in therapy, she wouldn't do anything when the weekends came around. She wouldn't participate in any family activities, not even going to church, which she used to enjoy. She would just sit on the chair all day, and there was nothing we could do about it.

"Time for supper, Nadya. Come to the table," I called her. She would not move. I made my way to the couch and leaned over, telling her again to come to the table. She yelled and told me to stop talking to her.

"Nadya, I'm only telling you that it is time to eat. Once everyone is finished and dinnertime is over, you will not be allowed to eat. Come on now, sweetie, let's go."

She reluctantly came to the table, but it started taking more and more effort to get her to do so. On weekends, she woke up at six a.m., went to the couch, and slept there all day. She got angry when I told her she needed to get up, get dressed, and brush her teeth.

"No. You can't tell me what to do!" she screamed.

I tried to explain that her body needed to move to keep her muscles strong. "Emily is coming to take you to the pet store today," I added, referring to her mentor from the Wraparound Program.

"I'm not going with her. You can't make me, so don't even think about it!" she barked at me.

"You have to go, just for a little while."

"Don't talk to me," she huffed, and turned away. I couldn't stand watching her lie on the couch sleeping. I tried to sit down next to her, and she quickly moved her legs to block me.

"I know what you're doing! You're making me mad, that's what you're doing. Go away!" she yelled.

If I persisted, her voice got even louder.

"Didn't I tell you not to talk to me?" she growled. I didn't know what to do when my daughter spoke to me like this. I walked away mouthing some choice swear words to myself. Karl was in our bedroom, watching a movie on his computer.

"Now what, Lori?" he asked when he saw me enter in a huff.

"*Now what?*" I echoed. "The same damn thing, that's what. I can't stand her lying around doing nothing! Delaney was emptying out the dishwasher, I was doing laundry, and Nadya wouldn't budge. She refused to help in the least. I can't stand it anymore," I continued. "She is so defiant and oppositional. She is getting worse, don't you think?"

"Yeah, she sure is," he replied. "Just leave her alone," he advised, but I had other ideas.

"Where are you going, Lori?" he called after me as I headed back out of the room.

"I'm taking the cushions off the couch!" I walked into the family room and told Nadya that she was no longer allowed to stay on the couch. I took a breath and started to take the cushions off.

"Nadya, these will be in our room now," I said, bracing myself.

She started wailing. "Noooooo!"

Nadya got up off the couch and pulled the cushion back out of my arms. I told her I would put them back on if she got up and got dressed. She glared at me and instead made her way to the overstuffed chair across from the couch and got under a blanket. The doorbell rang. I had lost all track of time. It was her mentor Emily, coming to take her on her weekend outing.

"Nadya won't get dressed today," I explained to Emily, hoping she could help. We had both been struggling to get Nadya to do anything for weeks.

"Nadya, why don't I help you get some clean clothes on?" Emily tried. "I will take you to the pet store where you volunteered. Remember that bird that sits on your finger? I bet that bird misses you."

"I'm not going anywhere with you," Nadya replied from under the covers.

"Nadya, you have to leave the house. We can go get an ice cream cone afterwards," Emily promised. This routine had always worked before, but now Nadya was silent.

I approached the chair and tried to lift her up, but she gouged my arm with her nails until I let go.

"Nadya, we cannot use hurting hands," Emily quickly reminded her, but Nayda said nothing. No matter how hard we bribed, she would not move. I took the cushion straight out from underneath her. I only dared to make this move because Emily was there, and I could count on her to help me if things escalated. Nadya stuck her face deep into the seam where the arm and back of the chair connected. She didn't budge. She stayed there for four hours. Emily finally left. I went upstairs, got Delaney, and went shopping.

After ruling out that her medication was causing the lethargy, I was at a loss. Nadya simply refused to move, at all. She didn't even watch TV; she either slept or played on her iPod. From the time she came home from school on Friday afternoon until late Sunday night, she was firmly planted in that chair, only getting up to eat and use the bathroom.

I tried to remind myself that it was just another one of the backward slides we periodically experienced, despite all the progress she had made. But even so, it was disheartening to see my daughter not want to do *anything*—not even move. Doesn't every parent just want to see their child display some kind of motivation? Have some interests or goals? Nadya had none—not even close. I would look at her sitting with her head buried in the corner of the couch, only her legs and torso visible, and wonder what kind of future she would have. What kind of future would we all have? How would she ever be able to hold down a job or support herself? How could she ever have any degree of independence?

The reality was becoming clearer with each passing day: Nadya would probably never be able to live an independent life as an adult. She still didn't understand so many basic things—time, money, food preparation, or even crossing the street safely. Taking care of her own hygiene was a major issue. She wouldn't even change her underwear if I didn't lay it out for her every day along with her socks, shirt, and pants. I finally decided I was no longer going to do these basic things for her. If she could do them at Genesee Lake School, she could do them here. If she did not want to shower but once a week, so be it. If she would not change her clothes, she could go to school with the same thing on. As horrible as it sounds, I had to do it. She needed to learn to care for her hygiene if she were ever to live anywhere other than our house.

Like any parents, we wanted what was best for our daughter, and that meant considering options for assisted living once she finished school. This new reality consumed my every waking thought. Would it be a group home? An independent living facility? Maybe a supervised apartment with other people like her? How would she interact with older male residents? I worried that if she was combative, or had a rage or attacked another emotionally disabled child, she wouldn't be allowed to stay in such facilities. Where would that leave us? I saw my daughter, how mentally disabled she was, and thought, *Oh, my God, I can't have her end up in a psychiatric institution. Not after all this. Not after everything we have been through.*

As Nadya gets older, it will only become increasingly difficult for us to find a suitable home for her. Karl and I are in our mid-fifties, and we can't take care of her every need forever. We have dreams of retiring in the Southwest—hopefully New Mexico. But the question remains: How can we leave her? She has to have a life outside of just sitting on our couch all day. We want so much for her to have that life, but it remains elusive.

One day, I went into the bathroom, locked myself in a stall, and cried.

"I am so sad seeing what she is becoming now," I texted Karl. I chewed my lip over the fact that despite all the best treatments we had obtained for our daughter, she would remain seriously disabled for the rest of her life.

"She has problems with so many basic things—even language. How can we send her to high school?"

Karl and I texted back and forth and then discussed it more that evening, debating the pros and cons of our situation, but there were no easy answers.

I still struggled with my own issues, too. Some days at work I felt like I had some atypical version of PTSD. Once, when I heard a coworker start yelling in another room, I immediately became sweaty and shaky, my breathing quickening. I was genuinely afraid to come out of my office. My boss had to come in and explain to me that it was just a confrontation between two of my coworkers and one of them had lost their temper, but that it was nothing to be afraid of.

"It's okay, Lori. Everybody's calmed down now," he said.

"God, that scared me. It scared me so much," I cried. The pieces, the connections, fell together in an instant. "I can't be around people who are angry—I panic because of everything that's happened at home. I'm sorry, I just . . . reacted." Years of exhaustion from holding Nadya down while she raged and hit had stayed with me, despite the fact that such meltdowns were rare lately, and in moments like this, I realized how much of an impact those violent outbursts had made on my psyche.

Later that night, Karl consoled me. "It's okay, Lori. It's understandable that you're so on edge considering the years of abuse you've endured."

I sighed into his body as I let the last of the tears fall. He was right. I couldn't pretend I had escaped the trauma unscathed.

CHAPTER 18
A LOVE CONNECTION

When we adopted Nadya, we had no idea her disabilities would be so severe. We had been prepared for her to have a learning disability, but we were not prepared for the reality that she would be dependent on us for the rest of her life. Sometimes I mourn the future she can never have because of the horrible things that were done to her when she was a baby, and I have to remind myself that she wouldn't have had any of this support in Russia. She would have aged out of the orphanage system at seventeen, if she hadn't run away before then (as many children do, ending up living on the streets). I've read that only ten percent of kids that age out of orphanages in Russia "make it"—meaning that they lead a normal life. The other ninety percent turn to drugs, alcohol, crime, and prostitution. Many get caught up in sex trafficking, and disproportionate numbers tragically commit suicide. This would not happen to our Nadya. Despite our lives often feeling like one step forward and two steps back, there had truly been profound progress in the years since bringing Nadya home.

One day, Nadya and I were sitting at the breakfast bar

eating sunflower seeds together.

"You know, Nadya," I began. "You have come a long way. Do you know what that means?"

"No," she shook her head.

"It means that you've gotten so much better," I explained. "Do you remember how a long time ago, even last year, you used to hit and bite and kick and scratch and slam doors . . ." My voice trailed off as she looked at me quizzically. "You remember that, right?"

She nodded.

"Well, you don't do that anymore. You've come a long way."

Nadya looked at me and paused. "Why? You want some more?"

I looked back at her with wide eyes. "No!" I said. "I do *not* want to go back there!"

And then we both burst into giggles. Her sense of humor made me feel close to her. Her ability to make a joke about her behavior showed me that even *she* knew how much she had grown—that she understood where she was, and indeed, how far she had come. The days when I thought I wouldn't survive the terror and anxiety felt like they had finally passed. Here I was and here we were—we had made it.

One summer night, we went to the Wisconsin State Fair to see one of our favorite Christian bands, MercyMe. Nadya loved their songs and was truly happy watching them perform. She rested her head against my shoulder as we took in the sounds wafting to us from the stage. We all giggled at the powdered sugar that was on our faces from the funnel cakes that Karl had gotten us. Those precious, sweet moments melted every fiber of my being. I took it all in. *She feels safe with me*, I marveled. It was something I had worked toward for over seven years. Now here she was, peaceful and enjoying the summer night in this beautiful moment that I wanted to capture in its perfection.

I knew these tender moments were my lifeline and her lifeline. This was my umbilical cord that she could attach to, that would nurture her where her birth mom had been unable, and it would be there always. This was what I needed to focus on. These were the moments that made it all worth it. It would be so easy to get lost in all the other stuff happening around us, last week or next week, so easy to worry about things that weren't right now. But I wanted to be present in that moment. I held Nadya's hand as she nuzzled into me and I reveled in her affection. I looked up to the stars and thanked God for this wonderful night, hugging her closer. The trust and affection she showed me in moments like these made me feel I had done it—that I had mothered this girl in the right way, that I had helped her begin to heal. A long road still stretched out before us, but I knew we were heading in the right direction.

Nadya is a beautiful girl and a beautiful soul—a soul that longed for attention at the beginning of life. I think about how she must have lain crying in a run-down Russian orphanage when she was just days old, with no one there to pick her up. I wonder how many hours, or even days, went by without her soiled diaper being changed. She arrived in this world longing to make a connection with an adult who would care for her, and yet in her tiniest, most fragile state, she was met only with neglect and abuse. For nearly ten years, no one comforted her when she had a bad dream, or told her they would turn her pillow over to give her good dreams. Now I see a girl who has learned how to laugh, who has experienced what it feels like to be happy. Two Russian orphanages nearly swallowed her up, and our family rescued her from the dark fate she faced there. Now, she makes my heart melt when she holds my hand and brings it to her face, nuzzling me while we watch TV together. She is silly and witty and makes me laugh. She is an amazing artist and it scares me to think how close the world came to never glimpsing her talents at all.

My Nadya. She has gorgeous blond hair, beautiful cheekbones, a perfect nose, crystal blue eyes, and full pink lips. I search deeply in those blue eyes when she is lying next to me and I wish I could have been there for her when she was a baby. I pull her closer to me while she sleeps peacefully. She feels loved, she feels safe, and I feel blessed that God chose me to take care of her, even though there are times when I feel like I am not good enough. Maybe another woman would have done a better job than I have, but God entrusted me and my family with Nadya, and he guided us through the tangled web of early childhood trauma and RAD. We have so much to be grateful for.

She is almost seventeen, and the long term is now upon us. All these years, I reached out to her and kept reaching out to make a love connection. God gave me the will, and Nadya urged me unknowingly to never give up on her. Our future may not look like what I thought it would when we adopted her, but when I hold her in my arms, I think, *We have made it. We have made a love connection.*

EPILOGUE

Every day I remind myself that Nadya's middle name is Hope. And the truth is that the world runs on hope—for everybody. Without hope, there is nothing. It's a simple idea that all people rely on, and our little family is no different. No matter what, I will always have hope in my heart for my little girl. Even on my darkest days, I knew hope was right around the corner, ready to pick me up when all seemed lost. I wanted Nadya to feel that hope as well.

It's not perfect all the time, but you can say that about *all* kids. Even kids who don't have attachment disorders aren't perfect all the time, so like all parents, I'll take the sweet moments when I can get them. Some kids, just like some adults, have more imperfections than others, but who are we to judge? No one will ever be perfect. When we see ourselves in the mirror, are we *really* seeing ourselves as others see us? Our society labels kids like Nadya "special needs," but don't we all have needs that are special and unique to us? We all need something different—from our families and caretakers and community. Some kids see the world completely different from every other kid their age. If we saw the world through their eyes for just a moment, we would see the world completely differently, too.

Sometimes we try to fit the world into neat pieces with labels and judgments, but then we have these special, unique children who make us snap out of that habit.

Special needs children don't judge like we do—they don't see the world the way we do. Nadya has never pointed out a disability. If she sees a kid in a wheelchair, she doesn't think anything of it, whereas a typically developed child might say something that identifies that child as different, or other.

Special needs kids like Nadya have a different viewpoint, a different way of seeing disabled people. They don't bully the autistic, the wheelchair bound, or the child with Down syndrome. Maybe that's the way God designed them—to teach us the beauty in *all* his children. To see as they do.

I never thought of myself as a warrior before, but now I believe I am. I might even be a *great* warrior. In the past, I fought a different kind of war—a physical one. Every day I would put on my suit of armor, gather my strength, and prepare for the fight before me. I never could have dreamed that my opponent would be this little girl, my daughter. She learned to fight from the moment she was born, while I had never fought a day in my life. I had to scramble and learn quickly, but I knew that once I started, my war would be won. I would never surrender.

I think back on all the drama and violence that our house has seen—there have been civil wars, world wars, and countless daily battles. Deep down though, my greatest war has been the battle of trust. Don't we all have reservations about trusting people at one point or another? Perhaps a loved one or family member, friend or employer, promised us something and then backed out. Broken hearts leave us jaded and unwilling to love again—everyone experiences that to some degree. But love is the most powerful force on earth, and no one can safely turn their back on it and expect to survive.

Love can change who you are, how you see the world. And a lack of love fractures your world so completely that it skews everything around you. Can you imagine living your entire life without being able to trust a single person? Not a one? That's a scary thought for an adult—but what about for a child? This is what my daughter faced her whole life, and this is what it did to her. She never had anyone to share her feelings with, no one ever took care of her, and no one took interest in her as a person. The first nine years of her life on earth were characterized by letdown after letdown. It's hard enough for an adult to learn to trust again after they've had their heart broken—how could a mere child handle this, moment after moment, day after day, and year after year?

One of the biggest lessons I have learned from being a mother to Nadya is that children who have experienced complex developmental trauma in their lives take a long time to rewire their brains into healthier patterns of functioning. Because Nadya's trauma came from a shattering of human connection, we learned over the years that the best way to heal her was with therapeutic, caring, consistent relationships. All the therapy and medication in the world won't heal a child whose fundamental problem is that she doesn't know how to have enduring, trusting relationships with people who love and care for her. For Nadya, love was indeed the most powerful healing. All those years ago when Karl said *all she needs is a family, and love* . . . it turns out, he was right. Not exactly in the way he thought, and not as quickly as he thought, but loving, consistent relationships have been the only reason that Nadya even stands a chance in this world.

For the first time in her life, Nadya has now experienced trust—maybe tenuous and halting—but it's trust, nevertheless. It has taken much hard work from her and from her family. She trusts me more than she has ever trusted anybody on earth, and that is a big accomplishment that has taken a long time. To this day, she still hides her favorite foods, like a bag of snap peas, in the back of the fridge because she is afraid that someone else might steal it. No matter how often I tell her that no one will eat her snap peas, she is not convinced.

"How can you be sure?" she asks, and then hides her snacks behind the bottle of orange juice. That is what lack of trust has done to this little girl.

This is the battle of trust I wage with her every day. She has lived with us for seven years and no one has ever taken anything of hers since she left the orphanage. Still, she clutches a favorite toy, like her iPod, and doesn't want to let it go. My job is to teach her that if she leaves it on the shelf, it will be there when she returns. She is always hesitant and searches my eyes.

"It's a game, honey," I try to convince her. "Let's play a game where you put your toy down because you trust me, and then we go to the next room. When we come back, it'll be here, you'll see."

She always shows such immense relief when we come back and her precious object is still there.

"See? I promised you it would still be here," I tell her—but we fight this battle every time. Sometimes she believes me, and other times it's hard to convince her. But no matter how tedious or difficult it is to teach her, I never give up. I am a warrior mother—a mother who loves her child. Even through those tough days, and there are many, I feel peace knowing that I'm able to make her laugh, that I've shown her happiness, and that now, finally, she knows what a mother is.

Nadya makes me a better mother. She has shown me a deeper side of myself than I ever knew I had. Without her, I would not have the patience that I have today. I would have never learned to love harder, and harder still. I don't know what my daughter's future looks like, but I want her to know that I have given it my all. I have never given up, and I never will. I am a warrior. I am a mother. I am *her* mother.

AFTERWORD

In 2015, Lori and Karl made the difficult decision to file a second CHIPS petition. They felt Nadya had reached a plateau in her progress and was in danger of backsliding. After meeting repeatedly with Nadya's entire team, they decided it was best that she receive the structured routine and professional support of residential care. At the time of this book's publication, the Hetzels hope that Nadya will be placed again at Genesee Lake School.

RESOURCES

WHAT YOU SHOULD KNOW ABOUT YOUR CHILD'S BRAIN: WHY EARLY STRESS EXPERIENCES COULD HAVE BEEN TOXIC, INHIBITING DEVELOPMENT

Adapted from a webinar series provided by Samantha Wilson, Ph.D., Associate Professor of Pediatrics, Medical College of Wisconsin. Available at *http://www.chw.org/medical-care/child-development-center/international-adoption-program/toxic-stress.*

- At birth, the human brain is only partially developed. Brains are built over time by growing nerve cells and making connections.

- Most brain development occurs after birth and requires experience to create neural pathways. The most-used connections become strongest, while the least-used fade away—this is important to understand when we think about children's early stress experiences.

- With repeated experience, stress reactions can become "wired in."

- Ongoing activation of the stress responses leads to biological memories and can physically disrupt early and later brain development.

- Stress that is limited, moderate, and predictable builds resilience.

- Stress that is chronic, severe, and unpredictable leads to trauma (and it's toxic).

- The brain generally responds to perceived stress in predictable ways:

    - Freeze—assess threat and lower visibility
    - Flee, or if cornered, fight—increase heart rate and increase adrenaline
    - Dissociate if threat is inescapable—lower heart rate, increase opiates

- About toxic stress: it is not early adversity alone that is problematic, but rather the absence or insufficiency of early protective relationships.

- Relationships are the basis of a child's stress response system.

- Children who develop in the context of toxic stress have a great deal of difficulty returning to a state of calm.

- If a brain was wired among chaotic input, behaviors are more likely guided by the emotional brain. Meanwhile, parent reasoning is aimed at the thinking brain.

- Words will NOT have a great impact on children who are guided by the emotional brain.

- In times of behavioral crisis, it is important to talk LESS, get physically LOW, move SLOWLY (if at all), and remain emotionally NEUTRAL.

- You must move your child from emotionality before you can "reason" and before they can learn. This often means delaying consequences.

- Remember to parent based on your child's EMOTIONAL age.

- Reconceptualize aggression: it's the sign of a scared child, not an angry child.

GENERAL POINTS TO KEEP IN MIND

Excerpted from *Supporting Development in Internationally Adopted Children*, by Deborah A. Hwa-Froelich, Ph.D., CCC-SLP (2012). Reprinted by permission from Paul H. Brookes Publishing Co., Inc (Baltimore).

- Internationally adopted children are a heterogeneous group. Those with a greater degree and duration of early adversity are generally at higher risk for developmental delay, behavior problems, and attachment disturbances.

- Cognitive/language skills, behavioral adjustment, and social-emotional development are synergistically interrelated.

- Attachment is the means through which children develop a stress regulation system.

- Secure attachment is associated with high caregiver responsivity and optimal child development.

- By nature of early relational experiences, internationally adopted children can demonstrate attachment behaviors that may be confusing to new caregivers.

- Some social-emotional vulnerability derived from early adversity may persist in subtle or overt ways, creating lasting effects on children and families.

- Later experiences with sensitive, responsive caregiving can compensate for early adversity. Warm, attentive caregiving is necessary, although not always sufficient, to promote secure attachment.

- In some cases, specialized parenting support to address effects of trauma/deprivation on the child's relatedness and stress response can facilitate family relationships and later positive development.

- Early childhood mental health providers (e.g., counselor, psychologist) can assist new parents to determine whether or not unusual behaviors/development reflect a cultural variant, temperamental trait, transitory concern, or developmental issue that is more chronic.

WHAT WE HAVE LEARNED ABOUT PARENTING A CHILD WITH RAD

Parenting a child with RAD takes time, patience, understanding, and the ability to love harder than you ever imagined. While every child is different, and each family's experiences with RAD and complex developmental trauma are different, these have been our top ten challenges with Nadya.

1. Severe language barrier at nine years old
2. Rages
3. Lack of trust, eye contact, and touch
4. Cognitive delays
5. Extremely poor social skills; lack of ability to interact with peers
6. Banging doors for hours
7. Screaming for hours
8. Demanding and controlling; constant defiance and inability to follow directions
9. Impulsivity
10. Silent refusal

If you share in some of the challenges above, the lessons and tools below could provide you with significant help.

1. Instill trust daily, and if your child is worried, re-assure her constantly that she won't be sent back to the orphanage, and that you won't abandon her. These are very real fears for some traumatized children.

2. Trying to develop affection is an important part of attachment, especially early on. I would put Nadya on my lap and just rub her leg or stroke her hair and look into her eyes the way I would a baby. This bonding is key for a child who might have trouble with touch and eye contact.

3. Be creative and use humor. Sometimes when Nadya was very upset and crying, I would put her in the shower and tell her the water was going to wash all her hurt, sad, and angry feelings away. I told her we could wave goodbye to them as they whirled around the drain. "Goodbye anger! Good-bye sadness," we would say as we waved to the "feelings." Sometimes it worked to calm her down, sometimes it didn't—but we were always looking for new and creative ways to help her regulate her emotions and feel better.

4. It is difficult to be spontaneous and do things on a whim with children who have RAD. Like all chil-dren, they need routines, plans, and clearly de-fined expectations to do well. Children with RAD just need these things defined even more clearly.

5. You must learn to control yourself and your emotions. You child feeds completely off of the state that you are in. When he is being defiant, keep reinforcing positivity. Though it may seem he is not listening, he is benefitting from your calm behavior.

6. Your child often cannot control herself, because she doesn't know how to regulate her emotions. You have to remember this. While most parents might lash out and discipline a child who is being violent or aggressive, this is counterproductive with a child who has experienced trauma. Your child is not "behaving badly"—she is acting in the only way her neurological adaptation allows.

7. If you have a child with RAD, you must understand that his or her brain is fundamentally different than your biological child's brain.

8. After your child has had a rage, you must try to reconnect with him as soon as possible, when he is calm, no matter how difficult it may feel. Talk in a slow, soft voice and tell him how much you understand his feelings, that you are not mad at him, and that you still love him.

9. Be prepared for your child to have some level of learning disability, and for the fact that he may never catch up with his peers.

10. Remember that while coping with complex developmental trauma is hard on you, it's harder on your child. She is the one experiencing the intense, painful emotions (such as rage and terror) and cannot control them or reason herself out of them. She is the one who was not cared for properly when she was little. Even when she pushes you away, she is craving your love.

ADVICE FOR PARENTS AND RESOURCES FOR COUPLES

If you are married and have a child with an attachment disorder, it is vital that you are supportive of each other. It does more harm than good to your spouse and child if only one parent is involved. You must be consistent in your parenting, and don't assign blame to each other. Here are some other ways to maintain your bond and parent your child *together*.

1. We started reading books and attending seminars (often online) on adoption and potential issues related to it as soon as we could. I highly recommend Dr. Karyn Purvis's work, especially *The Connected Child*. Her books will help you understand how a traumatized child's brain works. Dr. Bruce Perry's writings are also a great resource. Lastly, *Beyond Consequences, Logic, and Control: A Love-Based Approach to Helping Attachment-Challenged Children with Severe Behaviors* by Heather Forbes and Bryan Post is also very helpful.

2. Choose to see your child with a helpful, therapeutic perspective (i.e., not that she is doing this "on purpose" or "to get attention" but rather that this is an outcome of all the trauma she has experienced up until now).

3. Role-play a lot with visuals, reworking through problems and situations using pictures and drawings.

4. It was hugely beneficial for me to be in therapy myself, and I recommend that parents get support through therapy if they are struggling with a difficult adoption. While it may not be right for everybody, it was a key outlet for me for many years. You might also explore options for couples therapy.

5. Find a support group in your community for parents in a similar situation.

6. Keep a log of the good things your child does, even if they seem small, like saying thank you or doing what he is told the first time. You'll be grateful for the progress this list shows, and you'll find it useful to look at on days when everything seems to be going wrong.

7. Parenting a traumatized child is extremely difficult, and each of you must take care of yourself, too. Go on date nights, take walks, pray, get a massage, or

do whatever it takes to healthfully self-regulate. I like going to Barnes and Noble and cozying up in a chair for an hour to look at art books. When you are in a battle every day, you can become lost and nothing looks beautiful. Try to prevent that from happening.

8. Be prepared to advocate for your child in the school system. Know your rights as the parents of a disabled child.

9. Remember that you are not doing a bad job. You are doing the best job you can for your child. Remind each other of this often.

This might not have been the adoption you thought you were getting yourself into, but don't give up. Keep swimming in the whirlpool and keep your head above water. Sometimes that's all you can do. And remember: your child will teach you patience, love, and kindness beyond anything you could have imagined yourself capable of. You will be a better person for parenting this child.

REFERRAL INDICATORS

Excerpted from *Supporting Development in Internationally Adopted Children*, by Deborah A. Hwa-Froelich, Ph.D., CCC-SLP (2012). Reprinted by permission from Paul H. Brookes Publishing Co., Inc (Baltimore).

The following are times when children should be referred for mental health assessment:

- Parent(s) report increased distress, anger, or confusion regarding the child's behavior.
- There is little reported (or observed) positive emotional interchange between the child and parent(s).
- The child seeks comfort preferentially from unfamiliar adults rather than familiar caregivers.
- Parent(s) indicate that the child rarely communicates a need or feeling of distress.
- The child demonstrates poorly regulated emotions with reduced positive affect, increased irritability, and sadness.
- Self-injury that is worse in the presence of the parent, relative to other caregivers.
- Levels of anxiety that impede appropriate exploration in the presence of the parent.

WHAT TO KNOW ABOUT ENGAGING WITH A THERAPIST

While not all parents need to work with a therapist for their child, I recommend that parents of children with complex developmental trauma at least consider it. If you do think you will want therapy for your child, I recommend beginning your search for a therapist well before you bring the child home. The social worker doing your home study before the adoption should have some ideas about therapists who specialize in adoption. They should also be able to clue you in to local and state resources available to you.

Don't feel you need to work with the first therapist you speak to. As with all meaningful relationships, it's important to feel a sense of alignment and trust for the person you're asking to help your family. Ideally, you can conduct a phone interview with potential therapists and ask questions to get to know them better. Here are a few to start out:

- What is your approach?
- How does each session look?
- Will you also meet with the parents or is it one-on-one with my child?
- Will you give us behavioral strategies to try at home?
- Will you also be able to talk to his teacher(s)?

Inquire into the therapist's level of training and experience in working with children and trauma. Finally, try to find a therapist who will not only work with your child, but also help you navigate the system (i.e., collaborate with teachers and/or other providers like your child's psychiatrist). As always, remember that you are your child's best advocate. Do not be afraid to be vocal about your needs and concerns.

HELPFUL WEBSITES FOR FURTHER READING

These websites have helped us at different stages of parenting Nadya, and are also recommended by Nadya's longtime therapist, Dr. Samantha Wilson.

National Child Traumatic Stress Network
http://www.nctsn.org
http://www.nctsn.org/trauma-types/complex-trauma

Harvard Center on the Developing Child
http://developingchild.harvard.edu/resources/multimedia

Child Trauma Academy
http://childtrauma.org

The National Infertility and Adoption Education Organization
http://creatingafamily.org

International Adoption Program at the Children's Hospital
of Wisconsin
http://www.chw.org/medical-care/child-development-center
/international-adoption-program

Adoption Learning Partners
http://www.adoptionlearningpartners.org

Center for Adoption Medicine
http://www.adoptmed.org

Institute of Child Development
http://www.child.tcu.edu

Beyond Consequences Institute
http://www.beyondconsequences.com

Attachment Disorder Information by Arleta James
http://www.arletajames.com

Empowered to Connect – Dr. Karyn Purvis
http://empoweredtoconnect.org

Dyadic Developmental Psychotherapy
http://ddpnetwork.org

List of websites, books, and other resources
http://www.chw.org/medical-care/child-development-center
/international-adoption-program/toxic-stress

Alberta Family Wellness Initiative
http://www.albertafamilywellness.org/resources/video
/how-brains-are-built-core-story-brain-development

Helping Traumatized Children Learn
http://traumasensitiveschools.org

Mindsight Institute – Dr. Daniel Siegel
https://www.mindsightinstitute.com

Interview with Bruce Perry, M.D., Ph.D.
http://www.asktheexpertinterviews.com/drperry/index.html

ACKNOWLEDGMENTS

I want to thank Round Table Companies, Inc. for putting together such an incredible team to bring my story to life. A special thank you to Aleksandra Corwin for her unique talents in guiding me through this amazing experience.

To Dr. Samantha Wilson—thank you for your dedication and hard work with Nadya and with our family. You are such a blessing to me and to all the families under your care. I am grateful for those hugs more than you will ever know.

Karl—you are an incredible human being. Your love and compassion for the fatherless is what made me fall in love with you. You held me up when I was weak. Your arms consoled me when I was inconsolable. Thank you for helping me write our journey, not only in words, but in life.

To Mr. Jim Balestrieri, CEO of the Oconomowoc Residential Programs, Inc.—I extend my heartfelt gratitude for supporting the publication of this book. Thank you for believing in the importance of my story and its ability to inspire and give hope to other families who are struggling with reactive attachment disorder and early childhood traumas.

And to Nadya Hope—thank you for teaching me how to love harder. I love you.

LORI HETZEL

BIOGRAPHY

Lori Hetzel has been an advocate for adopted families and children for almost thirty years. She is the mother of four children—two biological, two adopted. She and her husband Karl are passionate about supporting disadvantaged children, and have made it one of their missions in life to care for those less fortunate. Lori continues her efforts at outreach and education for families within the adoption community through writing, speaking, and mentoring others. They live in Greenfield, Wisconsin.

ALEKSANDRA CORWIN

BIOGRAPHY

Aleksandra Corwin is an award-winning journalist, author, and book doctor. She has made a life and career out of asking questions, and loves the process of interviewing and connecting with people while helping their stories come alive. Drawing stories out of people and giving voice to the experiences they have inside themselves, but cannot express, is one of the best aspects of what she does for a living.

ABOUT ORP

Oconomowoc Residential Programs, Inc. is an employee-owned family of companies making a difference in the lives of people with disabilities. With service locations throughout Wisconsin and Indiana, our dedicated staff of 2,000 people provides quality services and professional care to more than 1,700 children, adolescents, and adults with special needs. ORP provides a comprehensive continuum of care. Child and adolescent programs include developmentally appropriate education and treatment in settings specifically attuned to their needs. These include residential therapeutic education and vocational services for students from all around the country. For those in or near Wisconsin and Indiana, we offer community-based residential supports, in-home supports, in- and out-of-home respite care, and alternative therapeutic day-school programs. We provide special programs for students with specific academic and social issues relative to a wide range of complex disabilities, including autism spectrum disorders, Asperger's disorder, cognitive and developmental disabilities, anxiety disorders, depression, bipolar disorder, reactive attachment disorder, attention deficit disorder, severe emotional and behavioral issues, Prader-Willi Syndrome, and other disabilities. Our adult services continuum includes community-based residential services for people with intellectual, developmental, and physical disabilities, brain injury, mental health and other behavioral impairments, and the medically fragile.

We also provide independent living homes, supervised apartments, community-based supports for adults in mental health crisis, day service programs, and respite services.

At ORP, our guiding principle is passion: a passion for the people we serve and for the work we do.

For a comprehensive look at each of our programs, please visit *www.orp.com*. For a collection of resources for parents, educators and administrators, and health-care professionals who are raising or supporting children with disabilities, please visit the ORP Library at *www.orplibrary.com*.

THE ORP LIBRARY

REACTIVE ATTACHMENT DISORDER

Loving Harder, An Unlikely Trust, and *Alina's Story* share the journeys of children diagnosed with reactive attachment disorder. *Loving Harder* is the true story of the Hetzel family, while *An Unlikely Trust* is a composite story based on dozens of intensive interviews with parents and clinicians. *Alina's Story* is a companion children's book and valuable therapeutic tool, offering a beautiful and accessible way for children with RAD to understand their own stories. The families in these books know their adopted children need help and work endlessly to find it, eventually discovering a special school that will teach the children new skills. Slowly, the children get better at expressing their feelings and solving problems. For the first time in their lives, they realize they are safe and loved . . . and capable of loving in return.

AN UNLIKELY TRUST

ALINA'S STORY OF ADOPTION,
COMPLEX TRAUMA,
HEALING, AND HOPE

ALINA'S STORY

LEARNING HOW
TO TRUST,
HEAL, AND HOPE

LOVING HARDER

OUR FAMILY'S ODYSSEY
THROUGH ADOPTION AND
REACTIVE ATTACHMENT
DISORDER

ASPERGER'S DISORDER

Meltdown and its companion comic book, *Melting Down*, are both based on the fictional story of Benjamin, a boy diagnosed with Asperger's disorder and additional challenging behavior. From the time Benjamin is a toddler, he and his parents know he is different: he doesn't play with his sister, refuses to make eye contact, and doesn't communicate well with others. And his tantrums are not like normal tantrums; they're meltdowns that will eventually make regular schooling—and day-to-day life—impossible. Both the prose book, intended for parents, educators, and mental health professionals, and the comic for the kids themselves demonstrate that the journey toward hope isn't simple . . . but with the right tools and teammates, it's possible.

MELTDOWN

ASPERGER'S DISORDER,
CHALLENGING BEHAVIOR,
AND A FAMILY'S JOURNEY
TOWARD HOPE

MELTING DOWN

A COMIC FOR KIDS WITH
ASPERGER'S DISORDER AND
CHALLENGING BEHAVIOR

AUTISM SPECTRUM DISORDER

Mr. Incredible shares the fictional story of Adam, a boy diagnosed with autistic disorder. On Adam's first birthday, his mother recognizes that something is different about him: he recoils from the touch of his family, preferring to accept physical contact only in the cool water of the family's pool. As Adam grows older, he avoids eye contact, is largely nonverbal, and has very specific ways of getting through the day; when those habits are disrupted, intense meltdowns and self-harmful behavior follow. From seeking a diagnosis to advocating for special education services, from keeping Adam safe to discovering his strengths, his family becomes his biggest champion. The journey to realizing Adam's potential isn't easy, but with hope, love, and the right tools and teammates, they find that Adam truly is *Mr. Incredible*. The companion comic in this series, inspired by social stories, offers an innovative, dynamic way to guide children—and parents, educators, and caregivers—through some of the daily struggles experienced by those with autism.

MR. INCREDIBLE

A STORY ABOUT AUTISM,
OVERCOMING CHALLENGING
BEHAVIOR, AND A FAMILY'S FIGHT
FOR SPECIAL EDUCATION RIGHTS

INCREDIBLE ADAM
AND A DAY WITH AUTISM

AN ILLUSTRATED STORY
INSPIRED BY SOCIAL NARRATIVES

BULLYING

Nearly one third of all school children face physical, verbal, social, or cyber bullying on a regular basis. Educators and parents search for ways to end bullying, but as that behavior becomes more sophisticated, it's harder to recognize and stop. In *Classroom Heroes*, Jason is a quiet, socially awkward seventh grader who has long suffered bullying in silence. His parents notice him becoming angrier and more withdrawn, but they don't realize the scope of the problem until one bully takes it too far—and one teacher acts on her determination to stop it. Both *Classroom Heroes* and *How to Be a Hero*—along with a supporting coloring book (*Heroes in the Classroom*) and curriculum guide (*Those Who Bully and Those Who Are Bullied*)—recognize that stopping bullying requires a change in mindset: adults and children must create a community that simply does not tolerate bullying. These books provide practical yet very effective strategies to end bullying, one student at a time.

CLASSROOM HEROES

ONE CHILD'S STRUGGLE WITH BULLYING AND A TEACHER'S MISSION TO CHANGE SCHOOL CULTURE

HOW TO BE A HERO

A COMIC BOOK ABOUT BULLYING

HEROES IN THE CLASSROOM

AN ACTIVITY BOOK ABOUT BULLYING

THOSE WHO BULLY AND THOSE WHO ARE BULLLIED

A GUIDE FOR CREATING HEROES IN THE CLASSROOM

FAMILY SUPPORT

Schuyler Walker was just four years old when he was diagnosed with autism, bipolar disorder, and ADHD. In 2004, childhood mental illness was rarely talked about or understood. With knowledge and resources scarce, Schuyler's mom, Christine, navigated a lonely maze to determine what treatments, medications, and therapies could benefit her son. In the ten years since his diagnosis, Christine has often wished she had a "how to" guide that would provide the real mom-to-mom information she needed to survive the day and, in the end, help her family navigate the maze with knowledge, humor, grace, and love. Christine may not have had a manual at the beginning of her journey, but she hopes this book will serve as yours.

CHASING HOPE
YOUR COMPASS FOR A NEW NORMAL

NAVIGATING THE WORLD
OF THE SPECIAL NEEDS CHILD

PRADER-WILLI SYNDROME

Estimated to occur once in every 15,000 births, Prader-Willi Syndrome is a rare genetic disorder that includes features of cognitive disabilities, problem behaviors, and, most pervasively, chronic hunger that leads to dangerous overeating and its life-threatening consequences. *Insatiable: A Prader-Willi Story* and its companion comic book, *Ultra-Violet: One Girl's Prader-Willi Story*, draw on dozens of intensive interviews to offer insight into the world of those struggling with Prader-Willi Syndrome. Both books tell the fictional story of Violet, a vivacious young girl born with the disorder, and her family, who—with the help of experts—will not give up their quest to give her a healthy and happy life.

INSATIABLE
A PRADER-WILLI STORY

ULTRA-VIOLET
ONE GIRL'S PRADER-WILLI STORY

Also look for books on children and psychotropic medications coming soon!

CPSIA information can be obtained at www.ICGtesting.com
Printed in the USA
LVOW04s0346101015

457638LV00001B/1/P